SOUND OF THE BEAST

ALSO BY DONNA-MICHELLE ST. BERNARD

Cake
Gas Girls
Indian Act: Residential School Plays (editor)
A Man A Fish
Refractions: Scenes (editor, with Yvette Nolan)
Refractions: Solo (editor, with Yvette Nolan)

SOUND OF THE BEAST
DONNA-MICHELLE ST. BERNARD
A.K.A. BELLADONNA THE BLEST

PLAYWRIGHTS CANADA PRESS
TORONTO

For professional or amateur production rights, please contact:
Michael Petrasek, Kensington Literary Representation
34 St. Andrew Street, Toronto, ON M5T 1K6
416.848.9648, kensingtonlit@rogers.com

LIBRARY AND ARCHIVES CANADA CATALOGUING IN PUBLICATION
Title: Sound of the beast / Donna-Michelle St. Bernard.
Names: St. Bernard, Donna-Michelle, author.
Description: A play.
Identifiers: Canadiana (print) 20200235184 | Canadiana (ebook)
  20200235222 | ISBN 9780369100764 (softcover)
  | ISBN 9780369100771 (PDF) | ISBN 9780369100788 (EPUB)
  | ISBN 9780369100795 (Kindle)
Classification: LCC PS8637.A4525 S68 2020 | DDC C812/.6—dc23

Playwrights Canada Press operates on Mississaugas of the Credit, Wendat, Anishinaabe, Métis, and Haudenosaunee land. It always was and always will be Indigenous land.

We acknowledge the financial support of the Canada Council for the Arts—which last year invested $153 million to bring the arts to Canadians throughout the country—the Ontario Arts Council (OAC), Ontario Creates, and the Government of Canada for our publishing activities.

As ever, respect to God, Mom and Kern.
But this one's for Hasty.

PLAYLIST

IT HAPPENED
BY KERN ALBERT

Here's the question I hear every time (Every. Time.) I'm in a lobby or gathering space after a performance of *Sound of the Beast* by Donna-Michelle St. Bernard: "How much of that was real?"

* * *

Being in a Black body is like . . .

I don't know who killed Joshua Brown. I know he testified against a police officer. The officer was on trial for murder. I know that during his testimony he broke down. A noteworthy and lasting image of that trial was the comfort and compassion afforded in generous display to the guilty officer—a hug by the presiding judge. The same comfort and compassion was not publicly awarded to Joshua as he did a brave and scary thing for a Black man in his position, his civic duty. Though the police officer was given a ten-year sentence, I know the verdict is being appealed. I know a major witness will not be on the stand the second go round, because dead men can't testify.

I don't know if Kalief Browder was sexually assaulted in jail. I know he spent three years there. I know he spent two of those years in solitary confinement. Pretrial. I know he was twenty-two when he died. He committed suicide in his mother's home two years after being released from prison. I know he was accused of stealing a backpack. I know he refused to plead guilty to that theft, even though that plea would have secured his release with time served. So, the authorities kept him in jail. He was eventually released because the prosecutor decided there really wasn't enough evidence to try the case after all—but apparently enough evidence to hold him in Rikers Island jail for three years. Pretrial. I don't know if there is a direct line from being unjustly accused to the torture of solitary confinement to the possibility of sexual exploitation to the finality of suicide. I don't know what the average cost of a backpack is. I never googled it.

I don't know if Dafonte Miller was a thief. There was no trial to determine the veracity of that accusation. I know that he's blind in one eye because, without a trial, a judgment was made and executed by a law-enforcement officer and his brother. I know that the initial extrajudicial judgment was backed and sanctioned in the court of public opinion. Case closed. However, to the surprise of many Black people, an actual court eventually decided to hear this case. Maybe some kind of justice will be meted out, finally, but Miller still has only one eye and maybe some brain damage, but who can truly say? I can say that the accused brothers are the sons of a father who is also in law enforcement. I can say that there is at least anecdotal evidence that law-enforcement officers protect their own. I mean, why wouldn't they? That's what any family, any brotherhood would do, right?

(Wouldn't you know, precisely while I'm writing this . . . George Floyd.)

This is what being in a Black body is like. I get tired carrying around the weight of names. It is good to know that it is a shared burden, though. It is useful to know that sharing a thing acknowledges its existence, and if a thing exists, then it's real. But besides all that, I was there for the events of *Sound of the Beast*. I was there. The thing exists.

It's all real.

I wanted to write this introduction because in order to fully realize the depth of the work, it's important to understand how some elements of Blackness function. Let us agree that there is no standard arbiter or measure of Blackness to begin with, but there is an equative shorthand that can be read by those who understand the language of the economy that is Blackness. It is a shared consciousness based on mutual—but not necessarily standardized—experience and interaction. As with a fiat economy, one must accept participation to derive real worth from a purely symbolic exchange. All currency is like that; it is a thing infused with "inherent" value and purpose. Participants agree upon its use to interact with others for the trading and acquisition of things needed for survival. Blackness is a currency.

* * *

So, it's early in the Global Pandemic. It's a time where "ewwww, they eat bats!?!" is still a thing unashamedly uttered in questionation. I have a friend. He's half Chinese, half Vietnamese, visibly presenting as Filipino, one hundred percent Canadian. He was born in Peterborough but raised in the Finch and Weston area. Most Torontonians are now confident of his class status.

By all conventional social indicators, he's culturally as Black as it gets; the way he dresses is "urban." He collects Nike brand sneakers; the phrase *Reverse Duck Camo Air Max 90* means something tangible and visceral to him. The way he walks is Black (with a purposeful gait, but on the balls of his feet, ready to break into a sprint). His music preference is "Black" (he enjoys hip hop immensely, but he *loves* R 'n' B). The way he talks is "street" (yes, there is a likkle hint of island in his cadence, between the general Jamaican of his hood and the specific

Guyanese of his next-door neighbours and oftentimes caretak-ers, while his mother was overnight on the factory line).

Early in the pandemic, when debate still raged over whether the virus originated in a Wuhan wet market or a Wuhan biolab, my friend felt the shift. He started noticing the looks. He began to be aware of the constant eyes. The uneasiness came soon behind. The cautiousness that insults. A legitimized reason to otherize. A dog whistle encapsulated in an uneasy shift of the shoulders. Accusation barely masked, so plain on the face. That most dangerous moment precisely between fight or flight— the "or."

My friend came up to me, an easy smile hiding this new, deep wound. "I've felt discrimination before, but now I know what being Black feels like."

* * *

I'm ashamed to confess that I am a spitter. I don't smoke. I don't have a reason. Except that I do have a reason: I'm full of phlegm, and since childhood I have decided that the best use (and place) for phlegm is as a forceful projectile, preferably striking a sidewalk. I'm actually not ashamed. I quite enjoy my little piece of sanctioned defiance. It's generally frowned upon, it borders on taboo, but you're allowed if you're a Tough Guy (because who's gonna stop you, really?). There are rules to being a Tough Guy spitter. You always spit with the wind, aiming down, and you never spit where there is a roof. But we're in the beginning of a pandemic and being a person of considerable learning, I'm swallowing. I've been swallowing for days!

Cue the public space. I'm waiting at a bus depot. Two fel-lows are smoking some twenty feet away. One has a dry mouth and every few seconds he spits. I stare. They see me, but think nothing of it, busy reliving some shared adventure, a joyous camaraderie between them. More spit. I am with the wind and my imagination feels the microscopic droplets of potentially lethal moisture wafting through my hoodie and sweats, so I approach. If my imagination can go rogue maverick, then so can I.

"Yo, you know what's happening in the world right now?"

One wears a quizzical expression.

The other, the spitter, doesn't quite hear me and steps closer. I halt his approach with my open palm.

He remembers. "Yeah. Social distancing," nodding.

I repeat, "You know what's happening in the world?"

Quizzical says, knowingly, enthusiastically, "Yeah, yeah, corona."

I go in, "All right, then you can't be spitting like that, yo." I'm expecting some resistance, some degree of defiance, one spitter to another. Instead, I get effusive and easy apology.

"Yeah, yeah, you right. My bad."

I was expecting a fight. The complete acquiescence leaves me impotent. I unnecessarily snark, "You swallow that shit!"

The guys, with their eyes, "What more do you want?"

I walked back to the bench at the end of the depot. They continued talking, less emotive, less gesticulation, less volume, no spitting. Both men visually presented as Asian. It strikes me as we're all sitting on the bus some time later—them, quietly in the back, me, contemplatively in the front—that their being Asian has just now occurred to me, but they probably felt pro-filed. Surely they would never believe that their ethnicity did not factor into my decision to confront them. I know that I did it partly because it's the responsible thing to do, and partly because if I can't spit, no one is allowed doing it in my presence. But I also know that if a face is slapped five times, when a hand is raised in the future, a reflexive recoil will occur, even if the full intention behind the hand is to offer physical comfort. Once you've been profiled, you create a template of instinct that sub-cedes thought.

Much later, as I pushed open my front door, I realized another possibility: maybe the Asian dudes did not feel profiled at all. As far as the exchange went, two guys forgot or did not recognize a thing and were reminded or made aware by another well-intentioned guy. As far as the exchange went, the profiling was inadvertent.

*   *   *

That's how it works. You are made aware of being Black, and then it becomes plausible that all things that transpire are informed by your Blackness.

My experience in a Black body has given me a very specific set of skills. If I were on the other side of the spitter exchange I would have plausibly concluded what was going down. I would have seen the profiling even if it was inadvertent.

But even without the benefit of my Black superpowers, that smoking Asian spitter had to know—as I did—that my call-out was sanctioned and fully backed by the powers that be. Whether or not my intent was pure, the systemic advantage afforded me by the social contract that framed my approach is, at its core, corrupt. So, the cognizance of my action is necessarily gangrenous, and it should be perceived as such. In that interaction, those fellows were at the bottom of the totem pole, we all knew it (and we all should know just how wrong that framing is).

* * *

In early 2020, an Asian woman was punched in the face by
a white male assailant. The investigator stood in front of a
podium and said, "We are seeing a rise in Asian-based hate
crime." This is a true statement, and worthy of acknowledge-
ment. Black people are not surprised.

Also true: in early 2020 a Black man was jogging adja-
cent to his neighbourhood in the middle of the day and three
white men shot and murdered him. The identities of the three
murderers are known. The motive of the murderers is known.
Months later, even though the addresses of the murderers are
now public, local authorities have not yet pressed charges, let
alone arrested them. Black people are not surprised.

Black people know well the incongruence of a system that
acknowledges a problem and denies the existence of the mechanism that creates the problem. Icebergs. Everyone knows the
larger, more dangerous bulk is always submerged out of sight.
Therefore, the insistence that all there is to them is what you
see is a blatant attempt to cause wrecks.

You may think you know what it's like to feel Black, but
you can't know what it's like to be Black. For authorities and
non-authorities alike to approach us as suspects, to expect less,
to demand more; the imposition of stereotypes, the steadfast acceptance of the generalities. The way we are forced to
operate and perform, all of it sanctioned by the wielders of
pervasive oppressive structural powers that govern our very
lives; lives that are simultaneously exploited as commodity
but deemed as things of little value. How dishonest, to preach
equality when the totem pole is still analogous of class and
race structure. How fitting that a most apt description of the

totality of white hegemonic supremacy smells like cultural appropriation.

If I was a smoking Asian spitter, I wouldn't consider the profiling inadvertent. What do I gain by holding that belief? What do I lose by giving it up? . . . I could lose my life by giving it up. I hold a tool of survival by holding on to the belief. *Sound of the Beast* is a brandishing of that survival tool, turning it into a weapon of self-reliance and self-defence. It is a declaration that a Black person cannot afford to assume the maybe good intentions of the oppressor. Is today the day the constant pressure relents? If today is not the day and I am not braced, I will be crushed. If the pressure relents and I am braced, then the not-oppressor (at least for today) is simply a little taken aback by how tense and ready I am.

* * *

If you're not Black, *Sound of the Beast* isn't REALLY for you; it's for us. It's a prayer. It is a communion. It is a lamentation as well as a rejoicing. A reconciliation. An affirmation. We know we matter. We know what it is like not to matter. That's not to say the play's not of value to non-Black people, that it is not worthy of time spent in contemplative pursuit or acquisitional desire. It's treasure! Once buried so deeply, but now expertly excavated. Unearthed with the precision and reverence of a Master Archae— (that was a test—did you wince when you read "Master"?) of an Accomplished Archaeologist. It is a treasure converted into a currency that can be traded for the commodities of acceptance and understanding.

What's more, *Sound of the Beast* is also a journey—an adventure of discovery.

And still *Sound of the Beast* is a map that sparks the journey that leads to the treasure.

If Blackness is a thing stolen and buried, then *Sound of the Beast* is a cipher. A clue that a map exists.

* * *

" . . . but now I know what being Black feels like," he said, an easy smile hiding this new, deep wound.

"Nah, fam," I replied. "That's like you shopping high-end wearing dusty clothes. You get scrutinized when you do it, but you always got the option to step your shit up. For me, that's shopping high-end. Period. I'm wearing my skin. Period.

"What you felt is just the exposure—a better view of the discrimination iceberg; a bit more revealed because it's closer to you. You still got that option to steer clear when you see it coming; we get *Titanic*'d every time."

Believe what you're about to read.

It happened.

Originally from Trinidad, Kern Albert sometimes reads books, sometimes writes things down, sometimes watches plays and most times sits in a corner and waits for something to happen. He likes doing all those things.

Sound of the Beast was first produced by Theatre Passe Muraille, Toronto, from April 13 to May 7, 2017, with the following cast and creative team:

Performer: Donna-Michelle St. Bernard

Directors and Dramaturges: Andy McKim and Jiv Parasram
ASL Component's Script: Tamyka Bullen
Lighting and Set Design: Rebecca Vandevelde
Composer and Sound Design: David Mesiha
Projection Design: Cameron Davis
Stage Manager: Heather Bellingham

People of color have always had our freedom of speech sup-
pressed in America; this is not new to us. We haven't been able
to depend on the government to protect our freedoms, and we
have had to protect ourselves from the government itself.
—Talib Kweli, "Free Speech or Die?" *Medium*

Freedom of Speech, that's some motherfuckin' bullshit
You say the wrong thing, they'll lock your ass up quick
—Ice-T, "Freedom of Speech"

I got worldwide family all over the earth.
And I worry 'bout 'em all for whatever it's worth.
—Dilated Peoples, "Worst Comes to Worst"

an unzipped hoodie lies on the stage, splayed out like a chalk outline.
a microphone lies on the ground upstage centre, nested in the coil of cord.
the performer enters.

LAND ACKNOWLEDGEMENT

the performer acknowledges the nations on whose territories she is performing.[1]

---

1   In production, this moment was used to acknowledge not only traditional territories and/or treaties, but also contemporary Indigenous struggles and meaningful acts of solidarity. Historicity + immediacy.

CYPHER

The cypher[2] is a circle,
like a sacred congregation
of spontaneous exchange,
ideas and energy the same
in that we're sparking from the flame
of this engagement,
relegated to the basements,
unpremeditated
and extemporaneous.

Welcome.

the performer lays down into the hoodie, arms in sleeves, embodies the story, breathes. the performer stands, zips the hoodie, puts the hood up.

---

2   An informal circle of creative exchange between rappers, beatboxers and/or breakdancers from which battle rap evolved. The term originates from members of Five-Percent Nation, active in early New York hip hop, and is said to derive from the coded messages that require specific knowledge to decipher. (Chuck D called

FUCK YOU

the performer picks up the mic.

My shoes say
Fuck you.
My jeans say
Fuck you.
My hood says[3]
Fuck you.
So you don't hear a word I'm saying.
It's just
Fuck you.
Fuck you.
Fuck you.

Cuz my face says
Fuck you.
My spine says
Fuck you.
My stance says
Fuck you.
So you don't hear a word I'm saying.

---

hip hop "the CNN of the streets," but not everyone has access to the channel.)
3   "I think the hoodie is as much responsible for Trayvon Martin's death as
George Zimmerman was." Geraldo Rivera expressed this not uncommon
pro-profiling view on *Fox and Friends* in March 2012.

It's just
Fuck you.
Fuck you.
Fuck you.

Mi ah di bad gyal[4]
Mi come fi mash up di place
Mi ah di bad gyal
Chuh, watch mi face

But it's your eyes see
Fuck you.
Your ears hear
Fuck you.
I ain't saying
Fuck you.
Now listen to the words I'm saying:
Fuck you.
Fuck you.
Fuck you.

---

4   Jamaican expats and immigrants were integral in the formation of hip hop,
informing the patois, rebellion and counterculture of the form. Reggae, as rebel
music, links to the evolution of ska into punk in the UK, paralleling the evolution of
rock and roll from blues—more rebel music rooted in Black pain.

I said your eyes see
Fuck you.
Your ears hear
Fuck you.
Man, I ain't saying
Fuck you.
Try to hear the words I'm saying.
Fuck you.
Fuck you.
Fuck all of you.

MICRO

Anyone feeling like I need to take it down a notch?
Like, hey, you came in at eleven.[5] We need you at a four.
We just got here.
Anyways, what's the problem?
It's no big deal.
A small thing.

Can I see your transfer?

Where are you off to today?

You live around here?

Do you have any ID?[6]

A small thing, no big deal
A few questions
A minute at most
No harm done.
Anyone wishing I would calm the fuck down?
Don't answer that.

---

5   "Well, it's one louder, isn't it? It's not ten" (Nigel Tufnel, *This Is Spinal Tap*, 1984).
6   Carding—police requests for civilian identification without apparent cause—is "a controversial practice that disproportionately targets young Black men and documents our activities across the city" (Desmond Cole, "The Skin I'm In," *Toronto Life*, 2015).

I'm not here to tell you how to feel.
I'm just gonna tell you what happened.

the performer floors the mic.

MYSPACE

the performer lowers the hood, steps into her bedroom, looks around.

This is the place that I dream from
Where I scream from rage or elation
Embracing my naked emotion
Unafraid of judgment or misunderstanding

One desk, 4 x 4
Lamp, chair, rug on floor
A little tattered but familiar
Scraps of my mind's insides
Scattered
On every surface
Haphazard
Or posted purposeful
Some low
Others higher
Words and images chosen to inspire
My best expressive self

This is the me that I have constructed
To remind the me that I am
Of the me that I hope one day to become

I say my space into being.
I raise these walls
From bricks of conviction
Constructing through diction
A frame at which I am the centre
And no one can enter
Whom I do not invite
Where the truest account is the one that I write

Immunity from prove yourself, move along or know your place
Impregnable blanket fort
Whose fortitude is in my faith
I'm safe here.

SLOW CRUISE

Have you ever been slow cruised?
If you have, then you know.
If you haven't, it's impossible to explain.
It's like . . . like this.

The cops are always out there, making themselves known
Nothing sinister, just visibility[7]
So when it happens . . .

It's a thing you know for sure happened when it was happening,
but when you try to say what happened, there's no happening
there to describe. This incident, which very definitely is something, becomes nothing. It is like a sentence without a verb.
They . . . blehhhh'd me.
I'm sorry, can you spell that?
No, I can't. And I can't draw a picture of it either, or point to it
on a doll. But this thing happened . . . happens. Frequently. It is
the frequency that gets under your skin. The perpetualness.

---

7   In defence of NYC's stop and frisk policy in 2015, then mayor Michael
Bloomberg said, "We put all the cops in minority neighbourhoods. Yes, that's
true. Why do we do it? Because that's where all the crime is."

the performer follows a slowly passing car with her eyes.

Each time they pass they are saying something.
Do you see me?
I see you.
And I know what you're about to do.
Am I gonna stop you today? Maybe . . . maybe . . .
Nah. Today I'll keep driving.
But I could have stopped. I could have.

It's a very grown-up game of "I'm not touching you."
And you don't want to get touched.[8]

So when you see them, you suddenly think, "Act like nothing's going on," which is how you were acting before you saw them, because nothing, genuinely, is going on. But suddenly you can't remember what that looked like, so you are racking your brain, trying to remember how fast you were walking before you saw them, and then you wonder, did I just speed up or slow down, and does that look suspicious, and is there a more suspicious looking person nearby I could walk past in order to become less threatening on the curve, and fair enough, I look like the type,[9] right? Fair enough. Cuz why didn't I wear a bow tie to the laundromat today? And all the while they are slowly cruising by.

---

8   "Profiling is itself a form of violence, because it infringes on Black people's ability to move freely and without fear in public space" (Robyn Maynard, *Policing Black Lives: State Violence in Canada From Slavery to the Present*, 2017).

9   "People from many different communities experience racial profiling.

the performer follows the slowly passing car with her eyes.

Do you know what I mean?
Have you ever been slow cruised?
If you have, then you know.
If you haven't . . .

You may say, "Just take it cuz it all serves a purpose"
And "If you never did nothing, why you getting nervous?"
Seems knee jerk on the surface, but it goes deeper:
Sound of the beast[10] is sound of the reaper.
Or the sleeper or the choke[11]
It's a taser for a toke
Grab the phone, then remember them three numbers is a joke[12]
And you're on your own when you hear that note
Cuz the system's broke . . .

Have you ever been slow cruised? . . .

(my own business)

However, it is often directed at Indigenous peoples, Muslims, Arabs, West Asians and Black people, and is often influenced by the distinctly negative stereotypes that people in these communities face" (2017 Ontario Human Rights Commission report on racial profiling).

ZED—GUY WITH A HAT

I think,
"I don't like those guys.
Those guys are always out there.
I'm gonna stay inside."

Then I say it,
"Zed, I'm gonna stay inside."

And Zed says,
"Whose streets are these? They're your streets.
And who's that guy? He's just a guy with a hat.
Here, now you're a guy with a hat, too."

And he gives me this. .

the performer takes a ballcap from her pocket.

Like I'd ever wear this stupid thing.

the performer mounts the cap on a spotlit mic stand, stage right.

---

10 "The sound of the beast" refers to the siren, the sound of the police, as in
"Sound of da Police" by KRS-One, released in 1993 on *Return of the Boom Bap*,
or "The Beast" by the Fugees, released in 1996 on *The Score*. The term encom-
passes individual police as appendages of a single monstrous entity, and draws

THE BOY 1—CAMPAIGN[13]

So there's this boy, his name is Weld El 15 and he's Tunis. That means he's from Tunisia. That's in Africa. You knew that.

So this boy is a rapper, and he goes around rapping. "Rappity rap rap. The government sucks!"

This man hears him, and the man says, "You're right, the government does suck!"

And the boy says, "I know."

The man says, "Hey, you're pretty good."

And the boy says, "I know."

The man says, "You know where you belong? On TV."

And the boy says, "I know!"

The man says, "I'm gonna run for office. I'm gonna fix this government, and you should help."

---

imagery from the political power that the Bible portends will rule over the earth in the end times (Revelation 13).

11   Excessive force has become personified by the death of Eric Garner, who was apprehended on suspicion of a misdemeanour and died when a police

The boy says, "I will."

So, the boy gives the man some cred. The man gives the boy a platform.
The boy helps. The man is elected.
Nice.

chokehold caused internal bleeding in his neck.

12   "911 Is A Joke" by Public Enemy, released in 1990 on *Fear of a Black Planet*.

13   I oversimplify. Weld El 15 was one of a number of young emcees rhyming in resistance to the corrupt regime of Prime Minister Zine El Abidine Ben Ali,

THE JACKET

BTW, I'm Donna. I do raps too.

So, we're doing this festival. Out of town, mainstage. So, you know, no big deal. Me and the crew—Zed, Jay, some local jabro-nis[14]—leave the hotel and head for the festival stage. Take in a few acts before taking the stage. Five minutes to showtime, I'm getting ready to go on. Zed steps in for the house DJ and lines up my beat. Jay walks up to me and says,

"What do you have on under that?"
"Tank top," I say.
He says, "It's gonna be pretty hot up there. You should lose the jacket." And he takes it off my shoulders.

I get on my game face and move forward, but this guy is stand-ing between me and the stage. The festival producer.
The producer looks at my bare shoulders and he says,
"You should put on your jacket before you go up there."
It sounds like a suggestion, but he's not moving.
Neither am I, for some reason.
Then the producer reaches past me for the jacket. Jay reaches past me to hand it to him. He hands me the jacket and they wait.

---

who was ousted in 2011. Notable voices in that movement include Psycho-M, El Général, L'Imbattable, Guito'n, RTM, Black Eye, Sincero, Kenzi, Wistar, Mohamed Ali Ben Jemaa.

14   Jabroni: an unimportant person. The wrestler whose job it is to lose cleanly

That's the moment, I think. The something happening. The
producer reaching past me for my jacket, Jay reaching past me to
hand it to him.
I think that's . . .

So he hands it to me, and I put it on.
I look over to the turntables and there's Zed, looking at me,
shaking his head . . .

So he hands it to me, and I put it on.
I put it on and he steps aside.
He steps aside and he says,
"There. Now you look like a nice girl."

Oh, that's it. The moment. It's that.
It's not when he told me to put the jacket on,
It's when I did.
I did, and then I got up on stage and did my song.
My song about how powerful I am.
And I am. I really am.

to another wrestler who is ascending in the ranks. The lowest class in pro
wrestling—in this instance, the "fams" attached to the crew. Popularized (in my
circles) by Dwayne "The Rock" Johnson.

BOMBSONG

the performer picks up the mic.

This song is a bomb, and I'm setting it off
Got a weight on my chest and I'm getting it off
You think you know me? Hardly.
I came to rock a beat, not to rock a party
I came to rock the foundations of civilization
Talking to a wayward nation
This song is the bomb that we're living in. Somebody pull
the pin

Down with music
Only subversives use it
For long-hairers and bong-sharers amusement
Everybody listen to the sound of one voice
Listen till you think that you've been given a choice

Down with freedoms
The people don't need 'em
Not with all the government's helpful interceding
They'll tell you what to eat. Tell you what to drink.
Tell you what to say, how to pray and how to think[15]

---

15   In 2019 Quebec instituted Bill 21, banning public sector employees from
wearing religious symbols at work—the compromised outcome of extended
right-wing agitation for an outright ban on hijabs. In the same year, the word

This song is a bomb and I'm setting it off
Got a weight on my chest and I'm getting it off
This song is the bomb that we're living in. Somebody pull
the pin

We safely communicate with slang and hand signs
I can't take it easy, man, I'm standing on a land mine
Click click.[16] I'm armed and under pressure
Sick. Sick. The harm cannot be measured.
Thick scars on my body and my psyche
And if you think you're worse off than me, you just might be
I know people who have seen hard times
Tying off or doing lines; I give them space in my rhymes
People renting out their bodies and leasing their souls
People railing cuz they feel like they got no control
Them hanging on the stoop cuz inside's hot as hell
Them that yell cuz they want to be heard as well
So when I say bomb, I mean the powder keg we sitting on
The freight train headed for the slaughterhouse we getting on
And when I say pull the pin, I mean it can't be hid,
I mean I saw what you did

"genocide" was used in the report from the National Inquiry into Missing and
Murdered Indigenous Women and Girls. A notable number of settler Canadians
just about lost their minds at the incivility of that language. Later that year, elev-
en-year-old Emmell Summerville was suspended from his Edmonton elementary

Somebody pull the pin

So, yeah. We're playing concerts, festivals, getting a little play on
the radio.
Cool.
Even cooler is when some kid comes up to you after the show
and says,

"I didn't know girls could do that."

Cool slash sad.

the performer floors the mic.

---

school for wearing a durag, a common head covering that the principal deemed
"gang-related." Oh, Canada.
16   The sound of a round being chambered. Also the title of another 54ology
play about South Sudanese minefields.

BUSTY

the performer walks down a city street late at night.

So it's five a.m. and six insomniacs have transformed the city
With glue buckets, paintbrushes, stickers and staple guns.
Me, Jay, Zed and three little jobbers[17]
If effort yields outcomes, the show is gonna be packed.
If those posters stay up forty-eight hours, I'm gonna be shocked.
It's not that I can't afford the $1 / poster extortion fee
That Grassroots charges not to tear them down.
I'm just not participating in that.
Fuck those guys.

Anyhow, futile task completed, I'm going to get a doughnut. I know
it's slow sugar suicide,[18] and I know you shouldn't eat in the middle
of the night, but I don't do five a.m. on an empty stomach. No one
else in the crew is interested, so I drift off by myself. It's hot and
I'm sloppy with sweat and glue, but I'm not worried about it.

---

17   Jobber: low status, unskilled, filler. A term used in labour, but also in wrestling, where it denotes the class just above a jabroni. Will lose the match, but
often not cleanly, because they "work" with more skill than a jabroni. (A clean loss
is a clear, uncontested pin fall, not clean is by disqualification, count out, "injury,"

This early in the morning, there's no one around; it's just quiet enough to really notice little things. Like how the birds you hear now are different than daytime birds. Or how that guy who seems to always be sitting in that doorway when you pass by is, in fact, always sitting in that doorway.

A block away from the doughnut shop, I'm waiting to cross the street and I notice that I can hear car tires behind me. I notice the car roll slowly beside me. The car stops. The window rolls down. Two pairs of shiny black shades are turned on me over straight slits of mouths.
Shades? Officer, officer. It's so dark out here I can't even read your badge numbers. Anyways, beneath the shades, one of the slits opens—slightly.

(as cop)	*Where do you live?*
(as self)	Nearby.
(as cop)	*Where?*
(as self)	Why?

---

interference or contested pin falls.)

18   The high rate of diabetes in First Nations communities can be traced, in part, to the reserve system imposed by the Canadian government. Prohibited from accessing their traditional diet, ration boxes containing flour, sugar, lard,

(as cop)	*What do you do?*
(as self)	What do you mean?
(as cop)	*Your work.*
(as self)	Why?

(as cop)	*Where are you going?*
(as self)	Over there.
(as cop)	*Why?*
(as self)	Why?

I feel like I don't understand the question—or is it the context?
I feel like there is a right answer—like this is a contest.
But I can't pull it apart, so I try to stay polite but not overly informative.
I feel sure there's a thing I shouldn't say,
But I don't know what it is so I am saying very little.

---

milk and salt formed the staples of a new diet. Haudenosaunee author Alicia Elliott writes eloquently about the epigenetic effects of generational hunger in *A Mind Spread Out on the Ground*. Incidence of diabetes is also disproportionately high in African American communities when compared with white Americans, but also when compared with Black populations outside of the Americas.

And I can see that it is becoming very annoying
And someone has to say something,
So I say,
"Is there a problem?"
And the mouths beneath the shades say
Without saying a word
That there is.
They say it with a lip curl—not a smile
But something shaped like one
So I ask again,
"Is there a problem?"
Realizing we have changed places
Now I have the questions
And they are the stonewall
And I still don't know what this conversation
is about
Or what it is I definitely shouldn't say
And then the cop says something he definitely
  shouldn't say:
"Look at you"
What, now?
"Look at your tits."
Wait, what did you say?
"You're so obviously a hooker."

the performer reacts—or doesn't.

Well . . . That went from weird to fucked up really fast.
And they're gone.
Because I guess I wasn't making an obvious hooker face or
whatever
So they decided I wasn't an obvious hooker after all
In spite of my obvious tits
"So what if I was!?"[19]

But they're already gone
So I'm just yelling to myself in the street
"So what if I was?"
Actually I'm pretty sure the guy sitting in that doorway
heard me.

---

19   "The conflation of sex work with human trafficking and sexual exploitation
has been used to justify law enforcement intrusions in sex workers' lives and has
empowered law enforcement to surveil, harass and abuse sex workers" (Canadian
HIV/AIDS Legal Network, "The Perils of 'Protection': Sex Workers' Experiences
of Law Enforcement in Ontario," 2018).

WILDIN'

the performer is tightly lit, centre stage. she stands perfectly still, hands at sides.

When a cop says, "Is there a problem?"
And you wanna be like:

the performer suddenly delivers one solid punch. her face: rage. an immediate return to stillness.

But that shit'll get you shot.

When a cop says, "Is there a problem?"
And you wanna be like:

the light tightens. the performer lunges forward with her upper body. her face: fighty. a return to stillness.

But that shit'll get you shot.

When a cop says, "Is there a problem?"
And you wanna be like:

the light tightens. the performer shrugs her shoulders. her face: uncertain. a return to stillness.

But that shit'll get you shot.

Listen, when a cop says, "Is there a problem?"
You better be like:

the light tightens. the performer is motionless. her face: neutral, tight-lipped.

Mm mnn.
Cuz you're not trying to get shot.
Mm mnn.

the performer shakes her head almost imperceptibly.

WORSHIP

woop woop:[20] *a police siren. the performer's hands go up by reflex.*

There's a reason why I flinch when I hear that.

woop woop.

Nuh unh. No, I don't wanna go near that.

(woop woop) / It's a call to prayer.
Mobile minaret. Throw your hands in the air
We been doing it this way for years
Come alert the second the sound reaches our ears
These things cut deep like incisions:
Politics. Culture. History. Religion.
Some of it is habit and some is decision.
Part blind flailing, part real vision.
Sacred book come down from the mount
Check the new scripture: Three strike count.[21]

---

20   KRS-One, "Sound of da Police," *Return of the Boom Bap*, 1993.

21   Of course baseball, but also the Californian three strikes law of 1994 that
helped template the "Clinton Crime Bill," which had the unintended (?) consequence of giving rise to the new prison indusrtial complex, the school-to-prison

(woop woop) / It's the O with the five[22]
Get to feeling like you're buried alive
Cops like a rock up on top of your coffin lid
Don't look shocked, yo, this shit happens often, kid
Keep yourself hard, on your guard against softening
Hands raised up to the sky like an offering
"All hail to the powers that be
I acknowledge your authority on bended knee
I submit. I surrender. I repent."
I give thanks in the moment when the boots relent

(woop woop) / Come on, come on. Sing it.
Gloves off. You soft. Come on, bring it.
You got me like shadow boxing the sky
Gone sightless with rage. Got rocks in the eye.
It's a matter of faith. It's a matter of fact.
The way I'm treated is the root of the way I act.
Thou shalt not use my first or last name.
This chick? Which bitch? That stunt? This stain?[23]
Thou shalt not let a nigger catch his breath[24]
If he says that he's hurting, you get so, so def[25]
Shoot first, then call for assistance
Blackness is an act of resistance
Poverty is revolution enlistment

---

pipeline and the exploitation of the 13th Amendment loophole that allows slavery in prisons. The law induces increasingly harsh sentences, culminating in a life sentence for any three offences committed by a person, regardless of seriousness. A life sentence for three marijuana arrests is not uncommon (Editorial, "The

ZED-BORDERS

I think,
"They're really asking for papers out there,
And people without papers get it rough
I'm gonna start walking with papers."

Then I say it,
"Zed, I'm gonna start walking with papers."

And Zed says,
"Why, are you crossing a border?"

Cuz Zed sees the big picture.

Three-Strikes Law for Sexual Predators Should Not be Struck Down," *Globe and Mail*, 20 Sep. 2012).

22   "The 5-O" refers to the police, derived from the 1970s American police drama *Hawaii Five-O*.

DEAR JUDAS

the performer drops to child level to address young Judas.

Some advice that I am reluctant to give to my son, Judas, who doesn't exist:

We don't want you to get got
So, here's what you need to do
To protect yourself.

Practise:
A vapid resting face devoid of emotion.
Having empty hands, and not needing anything in your pocket.[26]
Knowing two ways out of any place you're in.
Open a live-streaming app on your phone in less than three seconds.[27]
Saying "sir" without sarcasm.[28]
Buy a coffee, even if you're not staying long.[29]
Going wide-eyed to convey harmless, respectful fear.
Staying in shape in case you have to run, fight or drop down.
Speaking without gesture.

---

23   In 2018 a Chicago Police Facebook group was found to contain postings that propagate dehumanizing stereotypes of Black people—"Dindu Nuffins," "slugs for thugs," big, blaring n-bombs. In 2005 a similar investigation found RCMP officers circulating jokes reliant on racist views of Indigenous people.

Practise.
Practise till it's instinct.

Yeah, you can go.

the performer watches Judas leave.

24   The phrase "I can't breathe" became a rallying cry for Black Americans in
2014 after civilian Ramsey Orta released footage of his friend Eric Garner dying
in a police chokehold, repeating those words eleven times. In 2020, George
Floyd died with these same words on his lips, after almost nine minutes under the

So you remember that boy, and that man?

Sure you do. It was, like, a minute ago.

So the man is in his new office, and he looks around at all the shiny new tools of oppression he's inherited, and he's like, "Oh, these ones I like. These ones I keep." One day he hears a familiar voice outside his window.

(as Boy) "Rappity rap rap! The government sucks!"

The man says, "Hey, boy, stop talking about me!"

The boy says, "Rappity rap rap! Boulecia Kleb![30] The police are dogs."

knee of a police officer in Minneapolis.

25   A reference to Jermaine Dupri's record label, So So Def Recordings, which was met with widespread disapproval from hip hop purists who did not fully approve of Southern hip hop after the rising prominence of West Coast hip hop

The man says, "Stop talking about my friends!"

The boy says, "Man, you didn't fix shit."

The man says, "Hey, boy, you know where you belong? Jail."

And the boy's like, "Zoink!" and he takes off.

And this man, this friend of the boy, signs an arrest warrant and eventually sentences that boy to three years in jail.

Real nice.

as well as social influence from "traditional" East Coast hip hop.

26   Twelve-year-old Tamir Rice was fatally shot in 2014 by a Cleveland police officer who saw him playing with a toy gun. Some say the two seconds between getting out of the car and pulling the trigger were not enough for the officer to

STAY DOWN

Listen,
I live for this.
If you don't live for this, don't do this.

I live for this.
If you don't live for this, don't do this.

Stay down
If you're skittish, or petty, or need to stay pretty
If you can't move without decision by committee
If you think giving up your freedom makes you safe
If you believe if you behave they won't break your face.
Stay down
Don't get in the way.

Cuz I live for this.
If you don't live for this, don't do this.

I live for this.

---

apply sound judgment, and the Cleveland police department really brought the
hammer down with a ten-day suspension.

27   In 2016 Philando Castile was shot by police during a traffic stop. The last
moments of his life were live streamed on Facebook by his girlfriend, Diamond

UNDERCOVERS

the performer enters a local club.

So, yeah. The cops are always . . . out there, making themselves known and getting to know us. In the streets, in the schools,[31] in the club, at your door, on your Facebook page.[32]

They come in all kinds. It's not just the guys in uniform, way at the back of the club, out of range if there's danger on stage, within arm's reach of the door or the bar, so they can check IDs.

It's not just those guys. It's the super discreet undercovers in crewcuts and AC/DC shirts, skulking around the edges, talking. Just talking. *Hey, you come to a lot of these? You, uh, like to hang out with the socialists? The anarchists? Yeah, me too. Sedition is radical.*

After the show, it's the guys in the parking lot who make sure your audience sees them taking down plate numbers.

Reynolds. As Will Smith, a.k.a. the Fresh Prince observed, "Racism is not getting worse, it's getting filmed" (THR Staff, "Will Smith: 'Racism Is Not Getting Worse, It's Getting Filmed,'" *Hollywood Reporter*, 3 Aug. 2016).

28   On the last day of her life, Sandra Bland was taken into custody after the

When you get home, it's those guys parked in front of your house, or pulling up just behind you when you get home.

Not everybody thinks it's funny.

Not everybody thinks it's worth it.

officer who had pulled her over demanded she stop smoking, and then took issue with her tone.

29   In 2018, two African American men were arrested in a Philadelphia Starbucks shortly after arriving when staff called police to remove two "non-paying customers."

30   I condense. In 2013 Weld El 15 performed "Boulecia Kleb," deeply irritating the

ZED – GET HURT

I think,
"They do a thing, I say the thing they did, they do a worse thing.
If I keep bucking these cops, someone's gonna get hurt."

Then I say it,
"Zed, if I keep bucking these cops, someone's gonna get hurt."

And Zed says,
"Someone's gonna get hurt if you don't."

Cuz Zed sees the big picture.

*the performer writes a name of personal significance on her forearm in
memoriam—a family, friend or stranger taken too soon—in a ritual of
dedication.*

police, the conservatives and Tunisia's new prime minister. He was arrested again only
two months after being released from a prior sentence on similarly political grounds.

31   The School Resource Officer Program was active in Toronto schools from
2008–2017. In response to ongoing public concern about youth exposure to
intimidation and worse, Toronto's mayor and police board consistently insisted

WAR DRUM

There's a war going on outside in the street
Gunshots going off and the kids can't sleep
Can't speak to the grief. Can't stop to weep
Cuz they laugh in your face when they see you weak.[33]
Man, they laugh in your face when they see you weak.

One time, I walked into a bar and the bartender says,
"Hey, you wanna hear a joke about Trayvon Martin?"

---

there was insufficient data to support ending the program.

32   In response to Black Lives Matter Toronto's 2016 encampment outside of Toronto Police headquarters, the service's intelligence branch undertook investigation of Black activists and supporters through surveillance and analysis of social media engagement. BLMTO co-founder Pascale Diverlus remarked, "We know

BODY POLITIC

the performer accompanies the text with a physical score.

It's got a lotta parts to it
The heart, the lips, the arm, the fist
It's the body, the body politic
It's the heart, the lips, the arm, the fist

The heart wants what the heart wants
(Money, money)
Blood
Push it out.
Blood.
Run it through the system.
Blood.
It's running everything
Set the rhythm every other organ operate in.

It's the body, the body politic

---

that this happens. The targeting and surveillance of our communities is not new"
(Stephen Davis, "Police Monitored Black Lives Matter Toronto Protesters in
2016, Documents Show," *CBC News*, 3 May 2018).
33   "Trayvon Martin would have turned 21 today if he hadn't taken a man's
head and beaten it on the pavement before being shot." Right-wing political

They part the lips and impart the scripts
For lesser learned catechists
On the colonist's bandwidth,
Newsprint and sponsored link
Lacking in vigilance
Indifferent to the villagers
Infusing connotation
Through indoctrination propagation.

It's the body, the body politic

The arm flex and specks fly
From biceps, yes
Long lauded as the strength of the body
Since the Code of Hammurabi
Coming in
Laying Abrahamic discipline
It's the limb choose who getting crushed
Who getting cussed.
Who never getting up
Who gets the big cup
(Money, money)
Who gets to vote
Ayo-o-o

---

commentator Ben Shapiro uttered this untruth—his idea of a humorous witti-
cism—via Twitter amid an outpouring of community grief.

34   The "thin blue line" originated as a symbol of law enforcement forming a
barrier between society and chaos. It's meaning has become synonymous with

It's the body, the body politic

from a closed fist, the performer raises a different finger with each iteration of "singular."

Envision the singular
The civil individual
The singular
The singular
The singular
The singular
The multiple
Enlisted in the fist,
Again the singular.[34]

her fingers fold back into a fist, which is pounded into her opposite palm.

Who am I?[35]
Where do I fit?
Who am I?
Extract from the fist.

the performer extracts her middle finger and moves downstage, bringing it as close to an audience member's face as possible. she hold it for a little longer than is comfortable—for both.

---

the Blue Lives Matter movement—a grotesque, mischaracterized "response" to Black Lives Matter that became a defensive position and an extension of the "blue wall of silence"—a manifestation of police solidarity that inhibits officers from incriminating each other.

THE BIRD

I never do this. Well, I never used to. I've never been a fan
of the middle finger. The gesture seems crass and impotent—
people's reactions disproportionate. But there are those who
say it has its origins in the Battle of Agincourt, where French
archers, captured by the English, had their middle fingers—their
bow-yanking fingers—lopped off, and were sent back, useless.[36]
So, in that context, to raise one's middle finger is to say,

"Fuck you! Check out my finger. The finger you have not yet cut off,
the finger with which I will one day draw back the bow and let fly
an arrow into your eye, you filthy swine." A very efficient gesture.

Or in other words,

You didn't get me yet.
You didn't get me yet.
You didn't get me yet.

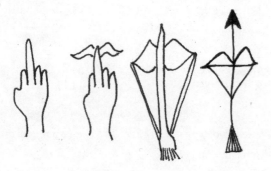

---

35 Beenie Man, "Who Am I," *Many Moods of Moses*, 1997.

36 A lie, but a good story that is oft repeated. In reality, the middle finger as
phallus goes as far back as Mesopotamia. As derogatory sign it goes as far back

ALIEN VS. PREDATOR

My friend Karen, who is a very nice lady, thinks I should chill
the fuck out.

"All this anger can't be good for your heart. Take a vacay. Go see a
movie. Live."

But it's not like that for me.
What kind of movie am I supposed to sit through?
La La Land? Sausage Party?[37]
Around the time we had this conversation, *Alien vs. Predator* was
pretty big.
I have not, and will not, ever watch *Alien vs. Predator*.

Some words become bound to each other
It's how dog whistles work
Will you indulge me?

the performer solicits audience responses to word association.

---

as Harappa. As profanity it goes as far back as 400 BCE Greece.

37   Surely more ridiculous movies have come out since then. Knock yourself out.

Peanut butter and . . . [38]
Tango and . . .
Starsky and . . .
Phineas and . . .
Pinky and . . .
Donald . . .
I would have accepted Glover, Duck or Sutherland.

Words get bound in different ways for different people
And once they're stuck, your brain finishes the phrase, meaning
the speaker's mouth doesn't have to.
So some words have an inherent prefix in my head.
You say alien, I hear illegal.
You say predator, I hear super.
So I can only assume *Alien vs. Predator*, a movie in which two
threats to mankind do lethal battle against each other here on
earth, is actually some filmmaker fantasizing a race war between
African Americans and undocumented Mexicans, and I don't
need to see that. Not even in metaphor.

Are you watching how they put the fear in you?
Go on, enjoy your movie, though.

---

38   The performer should feel free to use more relevant references to their
audience, and to use only as many prompts as feels appropriate.

I'VE HAD IT

the performer picks up the mic.

Welcome to the day that I say, "Hey, I've had it."
Maybe. Or maybe break another bad habit.
(B)[39] I'm about an arm's length away from my lunacy[40]
And that's a hair's breadth. I'm near death, as you can see
Mentally, I'm stagnant too much of the time
The most I feel engaged is when I'm building a rhyme
A ladder to climb, up out of Solomon's mines[41]
Where I know I am forgiven for the following crimes:
(B)(B) Keeping quiet when it's time to speak.
Feeling weak. Believing that I wasn't unique
Being bleak (B) when I'm surrounded by brilliance
Now is the moment to show some resilience.
(B)(B) Welcome to the day I rise above it
Stand on the battlements battered and love it
(B)(B) Welcome to the way I'm gonna do this
Every morning meet the sun coming up with two fists

---

39 The author uses (B) to denote a 1/4 rest in the meter, but understands that
each performer will bring their own flow to the words.

40 I am a self-identified non-compliant mad person. It's fine. I get by.

Watch me. Watch me. Something 'bout to happen
Gonna leave you out the other side your mouth laughing
And you'll be like, "No you didn't," and I'll be like, "Yes I did"
And you're gonna cry like a punked-off kid
Then I walk away slowly, and the soundtrack has this
black sound
And suddenly there's a helicopter exploding in the background
And I'm so cool. And I'm a big fucking star
And I'm coming for my people now, wherever they are.
I'm coming.
I'm coming.

---

41   *King Solomon's Mines* by Sir H. Rider Haggard (1885) follows European adventurers on an expedition in an unexplored region of Africa. The "King Solomon" referenced was actually Jedidiah, son of David, fourth king of the united monarchy of Israel and Judah, known for his copious wealth and wisdom.

THE BOY 3—RELEASE[42]

So that boy is in his cell.

The man is in his office.

One day they both hear voices outside the window.

The voices are yelling, "Free Weld El! Free Weld El!"

In his cell, the boy hears these voices, and he realizes, "That man put me in here, but the people are coming to get me out."

In his office, the man hears the same voices yelling "Free Weld El! Free Weld El!"

The man realizes, "Those people put me in here, and those people are pissed. This is not a good look for a man of the people."

And he lets the boy go.

---

42   "I'm happy to get out of jail and I will continue with my art and my music. I was freed thanks to the support, to my friends and to the pressure exerted on the Tunisian authorities." A statement from Alaa al-Yaacoubi, a.k.a. Weld El 15, upon his release.

Nice.

And I'm so cool. And I'm a big fucking star
And I'm coming for my people now, wherever they are.
I'm coming.
I'm coming.

the performer floors the mic.

FACE THE LINE

The idea of a protest is this:
Let's go out to a public place
And say out loud that we don't like a thing.

It's kumbaya.[43]
It's brothers in arms.[44]
It's fight the power.[45]
It's a little bit arts and crafts.
I've never made a placard myself,
But when I show up there's usually someone who's gone to town
and made ten,
So I've carried one.
Yeah, I'm one of those people.
Occupy[46] the park,
March in the streets,
Lay on the lawn of Parliament, people.

The reality of the protest is that it is all kinds of people.

---

43   "Kum Ba Yah" ("come by here") is attributed to the Gullah-Geechee people
of coastal Georgia and South Carolina.

44   Dire Straits, "Brothers in Arms," *Brothers in Arms*, 1985. Both a reference to
the fidelity of soldiers to a national cause and a unity call to embrace our brothers

The reality of the actual frontline is that you're fodder.

You're the wall of linked arms that marks the vanguard of a seething, agitated, uncoordinated mass of non-homogenous humanity.

You are little more than an arm's length away from the front-lines of a disciplined, coordinated armed and armoured mass of homogenous sanctioned authority.

Each one in their chitinous shell of bullet-proofing the dehu-manized uniformity that the uniforms intentionally evoke.

They're not people, then. They're power. And if someone hits the switch, it's coming at you, because you are the front line. And it's too late not to be the front line.

This riot-geared power front is holding the line. The seething mass behind is pulsing, pushing ever so slightly forward with its bodies and its will.

---

in our arms, to be responsible for each other.

45   The Isley Brothers, "Fight The Power," *The Heat Is On*, 1975, and Public Enemy, "Fight the Power," *Do The Right Thing* soundtrack, 1989, and rereleased in 1990 on *Fear of Black Planet*. Both anthems.

The guy behind me wants so badly for there to be violence that he is trying to make it happen. He is yelling stuff over my shoulder at the cop across from me, knowing that the cop will have to go through me to get to him, and not minding that at all. The cop across from me is ignoring him with inhuman stoicism. A drop of sweat escapes from under the cop's helmet and rolls down his cheek, glistening in the sun.

Huh. A drop of human sweat,
The salty water that human pores express
To relieve heat or stress. Huh.

The sweat draws a line down his throat, doing a detour around his Adam's apple and disappears into the depths of the sixty-five pounds of riot gear he is wearing on top of his uniform.

It's hot, I realize.
I wonder what's more aggravating:
One yelling idiot or sixty-five pounds under thirty-five degrees[47]
And I break the line.
I unlink my arms and take two steps forward.

---

46   Occupy Wall Street, which blossomed into an international movement performed and powered by progressive leftists seeking socio-political remedy for cultural, social and economic inequality.

47   Celsius.

"Hey," I say.
He stares straight ahead.

"It's hot," I say.
He doesn't move but the muscles in his temple say he almost
blinked.

"You must be so hot under all that gear," I say.
"Do you want some water?"
I hold out my bottle.
He doesn't move
But the muscles around his mouth say he almost smiled.

"I can't take that," he says
But he doesn't say he doesn't want to
I put the bottle away and I look at him for a second.

"I'm Donna," I say.
"I'm a real human person.
I just wanted you to know that."
He looks at me for a second.

He says, "I'm Jeff.
Ten years ago I would have been on your side of the line.
Good luck."

I'm gonna say thanks, but I don't get to.
There's a brief mechanical buzz in his ear
And his face goes all stoic again.

"Step back," he says.
"We're about to go."

I step back into the line,
Link arms again
And I'm part of the wall.
There is no more me.
The wall pushes forward.
I look across the closing gap between the lines
And Jeff is gone.
There is no more Jeff.
There is only armed and armoured discipline,
And it is in there throwing elbows just like the rest of us.
There's no more Jeff.
There's no more me.

the performer makes the "enlisted in the fist" gesture from "Body Politic,"
showing five fingers that fold into a fist, which is pounded into the open palm.

GIMME THE BOOTS

Gimme the boots. Gimme the boots.[48]
Uh. Uh.
Gimme the boots. Gimme the boots.

Turn the corner: there's a body on the ground
All slumped
Three or four more gathered round
Dark lumps
Kind of jerking, like now and then a great heave
Someone laughing, yeah, the one with the short sleeve
Headlights pass. Now I see their faces. Wait, stop.
I see the badges and the uniforms. Great, cops.
I turn around. Run, trip, fall, I see it all.
About to happen and I'm trapped.
Another witness

Thump
Sometimes it comes out of the dark.
One minute nothing, then the next it starts
Bright sparks of light from behind your eyes
And you're down

---

48   Rhythmically references "Gimme the Loot" by Notorious B.I.G., released in 1994 on *Ready to Die*.

Thump

Sometimes you see it coming and there's nothing you can do
And you just got to take it. Grit teeth. Get through.
And you wonder when somebody's gonna notice that
you're gone
And how long this is gonna go on.

Sometimes you think it's coming and you put up your hands and
flinch
Sometimes you're sure it's imminent
. . . And it isn't

Sometimes you're terrified
Sometimes you're sure you're gonna die
But tonight I just watch, and think . . . I know that guy
And in the morning we check the headlines
But it's like it never happened cuz it's one of those lives.[49]

Gimme the boots. Gimme the boots.
Uh. Uh.
Gimme the boots. Gimme the boots.

---

49   Marginalized lives matter.

ADJECTIVES

the performer makes an ongoing assessment of response and an unreasonable amount of eye contact.

Yesterday, a person was shot.
Yesterday, a person was shot by a cop.
Yesterday, an unarmed person was shot by a cop.
Yesterday, an unarmed fifteen-year-old was shot by a cop.
Yesterday, an unarmed fifteen-year-old girl was shot by a cop.
Yesterday, an unarmed fifteen-year-old girl was shot by a cop in Toronto.[50]
Yesterday, an unarmed disabled fifteen-year-old girl was shot by a cop in Toronto.
Yesterday, an unarmed disabled fifteen-year-old girl was shot by a cop in Toronto while pushing a baby stroller.
Yesterday, an unarmed disabled fifteen-year-old Korean girl in Toronto was shot by a cop while pushing a baby stroller.

Just checking in:
At what point did you start to think she didn't deserve it?
Which adjective was the tipping point for you?

Don't answer. Please, don't answer.

We're all just an accumulation of adjectives. Right?

---

50   The performer should reference locality in which the performance is taking place.

ZED — MURDER IS RUDE

I think,
"I love people.
Cops are people.
Why am I so rude to cops?"

Then I say it,
"Dude, why am I so rude to cops?"

And Zed says,
"You're rude? Huh. Murder is rude."[51]

---

51   A reassurance from Jahsun of Kalmunity Jazz Project, Montreal. A verified fact, though often omitted from etiquette manuals.

WHATSOEVER YOU DO

Whatsoever you do
To the least of mine[52]
To the least of mine
You do to me, too
You do to me, too

People shell-shocked. Sitting in silence.
Faces yard long.[53] Each one an island.
Hear ye, hear ye, let it be known.
No one on my block walks alone

Ain't got much. But I got eyes
I know a thing or two. Uh huh, no flies.
I'm only saying what we're seeing and we're sick to the teeth
We need a TRO[54] on the beast (I-I-I—say)

We not gon' stand for it. The weight is crushin'.
Get behind me, y'all. Start pushing.
If you can't stand, then start leaning.
You know and I know your life has meaning
And they can't take it. No, they can't take it.
And they can't take it.

---

52   Matthew 25:40.

53   "Yard": Jamaican colloquialism for Jamaica, or back home. "Yard long":
a longing for home. Thousand-yard stare: an unresponsive state indicative of
trauma, as observed in soldiers on the battlefield. Three-yard stare: equivalent of

Even if you're young and you look a little older[55]
Even if you walk with the gait of a soldier
Even if you've got a big chip on your shoulder
You still people.

Even if you rap about life in the street[56]
Even if they don't like the friends you keep
Even if you got a past, got a rap sheet
You still people.

Shut us in a box now.
Keep us on lockdown.
You be the hound and I'll be the fox now.
We still people

Whatsoever you do
To the least of mine[57]
To the least of mine
You do to me, too
You do to me, too

---

the above, acquired by prisoners after extended solitary confinement.

54   A TRO is a temporary restraining order.

55   "Contexts where Black children are dehumanized reduce the human
protections given to those children in two ways: making them seem older and

If he sell loose cigarettes, nonetheless[58]
If she sick and she off meds, nonetheless
If they can't form a sentence, nonetheless
None of these offences carries a death sentence

Crossing in traffic, nonetheless
Spray-painting graphics, nonetheless
Looking really ratchet, nonetheless
None of these offences carries a death sentence

Having a bad trip, nonetheless
Givin' you a little lip, nonetheless
Ain't supposed to have a dick,[59] nonetheless
None of these offences carries a death sentence

the performer floors the mic.

---

decreasing the perception of "children" as essential—each rendering them less
innocent and more vulnerable to harsh, adult-like treatment" (Phillip Goff et al.,
"The Essence of Innocence: Consequences of Dehumanizing Black Children,"
Journal of Personality and Social Psychology 106, 2014).

YOUR GOOD NAME

Some advice that I am reluctant to give to my son, Judas, who
does not exist.

Sometimes you're gonna get got.
So, here's what you need to do with your social media accounts
To protect your good name, after.

Post photos:
You with your grandmother, smiling.
You in a church.
You in a robe at graduation, smiling.
You at Comic Con, in yellow Power Ranger cosplay. Only the
Yellow Ranger.
You playing a team sport, or volunteering in the community.
Yes, you can post pictures with your friends—as long as they're
not visibly Muslim
Yes, you can post pictures of Snoop Dogg—but only if he is with
Martha Stewart[60]
Quotes from Martin,[61] not from Malcolm.[62]

---

56 In 2015 San Diego rapper Tiny Doo stood trial in connection with nine
shootings on the grounds that his lyrics about street violence constituted a con-
spiracy with gang members.

57 Matthew 25:40.

Try to project:
Potential
Positivity
Non-violence
Forgiveness

All right, go on.

the performer watches teen Judas leave. she may never see him again.

---

58   Eric Garner lost his life in 2014 because police suspected him of selling loose cigarettes, thus depriving the government of their tobacco tax or something.

59   Gwen Araujo (2002), Nevaeh Johnson (2003), Latisha King (2008), Angie Zapata (2008), Shelley "Treasure" Hilliard (2011), Julie Berman (2019).

60   Snoop Dogg was somehow sanitized by appearing with ex-convict Martha

STOP, FRISK

Stop stop, frisk frisk[63]
Look a little bit like. Risk risk
Ooh, cat looking like a strange fish
You strapped? Wonder what your range is . . .
I wonder what your range is

I once saw this guy get arrested for intent to break and enter,
Because there was a rock in his pocket.
That's wack.

Stewart on *Martha & Snoop's Potluck Dinner Party* in 2016.

61   Like this: "I have decided to stick with love. Hate is too great a burden to
bear." But not this: "I've come to the realization that I think we may be integrating
into a burning house." Or this: "Why does white America delude itself, and how
does it rationalize the evil it retains?"

BRUISES

the performer enters a mobilizing space.

We go on doing what we do.
We gather in places that feel like home and stay screw-face outside.
We take note of the patterns.
Every day, one less voice in the cypher
Every night, checking the news for familiar names
Silencing the questions we can answer without asking.
And knowing that we're going in circles
Unless we take the things we say in the basement
And bring them out into the light.
Truth to power.[64]
Strength in solidarity.

"Get it up, guys.
You know what's good.
There's a demonstration down at 52 Division[65] and we're all going.
All that energy you brought to the stage last night,
Today, we're gonna take it to the streets."

---

62   OMG, definitely not this: "We are non-violent with people who are non-violent with us." Or this: "Concerning non-violence, it is criminal to teach a man not to defend himself when he is the constant victim of brutal attacks."

63   Toronto Police's 2014 introduction of carding was derived from "stop and

(as some jabroni)   TAKE IT TO THE SKREETS!

"Yes, to the streets. I just said that.
Get into it, y'all.
Let's let them know that what we came to do is—"

(as some jabroni)   STICK IT TO THE MAN!

"Okay, first of all
I resent the implication
That women are not equally capable of wielding oppres-
sive power
But yes.
Stick it to the person, indeed.
Today, we're gonna get out there and—"

(as some jabroni)   TAKE THEM DOWN.

"Actually, I'd rather focus on raising us up. You see, the reciprocal
degradation of those in the institution and those in the working class is a self-perpetuating mechanism fuelled by our mutual
alienation from the core of each other's humanity. We need to
bring them the message, and the message is—"

---

frisk," a New York City police practice of patting down pedestrians for concealed
weapons, which was ruled unconstitutional by US courts in 2013. Both practices
are opportunities for profiling and harassment of people of colour.

64   The phrase originates in a 1955 pamphlet titled "Speak Truth to Power: A

(as some jabroni) DOWN WITH PIGS.

"Okay, wow. What did I only just say about cores of humanity?
Never mind.
Let's go.
Can we go?
Oh, we can't. Jay's late.
Of course he is.
Jay's always late. Frigging Jay."

the performer watches Jay enter, late, and approaches him, furious.

"Jay, are you for fucking serious with this?
Some of us are not fucking around here.
Some of us see this as a responsibility.
Get it?
Oh, nothing to say? I didn't think so."

Zed attempts to interrupt the tirade. the performer turns on Zed.

Quaker Search for an Alternative to Violence," and is good practice.

65   52 Division is a downtown division of the Toronto Police.

66   Grassroots collectives like Canadian Somali Mothers Association have con-
fronted police about the death of Abdirahman Abdi and others, challenging the

"No, Zed, he can stand there and take it.
Cuz he fucked up."

the performer turns back to Jay, closing in on him.

"You're a selfish prick, and you fucked up
And you probably won't even apologize until I
tell you to,
You deflated fucking fish lung.

Some of us see this as a responsibility.
Get it?
To mothers whose sons don't come home[66]
To brothers being disappeared in solitary[67]
To yourself. It could be you next, did you think about that?
Why am I busting my ass for your liberation?
If you're too selfish to show up for us,
At least do it for yourself.
Where were you?
Make it good."

---

use of force in arrests and altercations.

67   Canadian prisons have been criticized for an overreliance on solitary
confinement, administrative segregation, close confinement and structured inter-
vention units. Notably high rates of solitary confinement are recorded in Atlantic

I'm done. It's his turn to speak.
He doesn't. He keeps looking me in the eye
As he slowly takes off his shirt.
The kid's body has always been pale.
Now he's so mottled with bruises he looks tie-dyed.

I say, "Who?"

He says, "Who do you think?"

No one thinks of anything else to say.
Jay sits.
Zed scrambles him some eggs.
Jay eats them.
We go to the demonstration, but I choke on my slogans,
Because I think, basically, that I am a piece of shit.
I probably should have said sorry or something.

It's not that the concept of second-class citizens is shocking.
What's shocking is the fact that it is not shocking.[68] That it's just
reality.[69]
Shocking.

Canada and the Prairies, where Indigenous people are disproportionately incarcerated. Ivan Zinger, the Correctional Investigator of Canada, describes solitary
confinement as "the most onerous and depriving experience that the state can
legitimately administer in Canada" (Anita Grace, "Why a Federal Bill About to

"Who do you think?"
He says.
"Who do you think?"

Like, really.
Who did I think.

Take Effect Won't be the End of Solitary Confinement in Canada," *Toronto Star*, 15 Nov. 2019).

68   See Sylvie Mrug, Anjana Madan and Michael Windle, "Emotional Desensitization to Violence Contributes to Adolescents' Violent Behavior,"

Remember that boy? He couldn't wait to get back.
To his friends, his family, his crew. To the studio.
But before the ink is dry on his release, he hears that there is a
new silence in the cypher.
Cuz the cops just picked up another member of his crew—Klay
BBJ—for a pro-marijuana song called "Zakataka."[71]

Now the boy knows what need to be done.
But the boy has only just had some prison, and he doesn't want
any more.

the performer adopts the tight-lipped stance from "Wildin'."

Mm mn.
Still, somehow, he has to take it to the people.
What to do?
I mean, obviously he gets over his apprehension and rouses the
rabble.
But online this time.
From France.
As best he can.
And that's okay.

Journal of Abnormal Child Psychology 44.1, 2015.

69 "Research suggests that for people of color, frequent exposure to the
shootings of black people can have long-term mental health effects" (Kenya
Downs, "When Black Death Goes Viral, It Can Trigger PTSD-Like Trauma,"

We all do as much as we can until we can't, and that has to be okay.

. . .

Anyway, Jay called.
He says he's out.
He doesn't want any more. And that's all right.
He's done as much as he can, and now he can't anymore.
And that's okay.
That has to be okay.
So it is.

PBS NewsHour, 22 Jul. 2016).
70   In reality, both Klay BBJ and Weld El 15 were detained repeatedly, their stories coming to light through the work of journalists like Hind Meddeb, who was arrested for covering the story; Emine Mtiraoui, who was assaulted by law

HYPERLINK

So this one time, I'm having coffee with my friend Karen,[72] who
is a very nice lady. We're talking to these two little girls, aged
four and seven, when one of them says to me,
You can't even drive? How old are you!?
And I say,
I'm forty, little girl.
And she says,
No way! You're not forty!
And Karen says,
She is, but she doesn't look it, does she? Do you know why, little girl?
And I'm like,
Karen, NOOOO

the performer dives in slow motion to intercept her.

And Karen's like,
*Hold on. I'm helping. Little girl, do you know why she doesn't look as old as
she is? That's because Black people have maaaaagical skin.*

Fuck you, Karen. Fuck you in the eye.
That's that "Black don't crack" shit.
Shit that sounds cute cuz it rhymes.
That shit ain't cute.

---

enforcement while covering the trial; Lina Ben Mhenni and Thameur Mekki, who
defied other acts of silencing; as well as mobilization by Human Rights Watch
and the Committee to Protect Rappers.

71   "Zakataka" by Klay BBJ and Hamzaoui Med Amine was released in 2011.

Okay, there's a lot here, so I'm just gonna lay it out. Can I get a beat?
Thank you.

You all are familiar with the North American slave trade, in a general sense, right? Cuz that saves us, like, twenty minutes.

So. Back during slavery. There were some slave owners who were like, totally into it. And there were others who were like, "I'm not really into it, but I'll do it . . . for economic reasons." The more enthusiastic fellas would go and have a word with their gentler neighbours. They'd say, "What is it with you? Why are you so light with the whip? You're making the rest of us look brutal. Does it make you feel bad? Do you think you're hurting them? You've got it all wrong. You're thinking of them like people. But they're not like us. These ones have the strength of ten men. They don't crack. So put your back into it."

Okay, that was a long time ago. That's fair.

Much of Klay BBJ's work is boldly critical of police and politicians in Tunisia. "I blast the police because they're the stick that the system beats us with" (quoted in Sam Kimball, "Tunisia's Neglected Youth Find Their Voice in Hip Hop, Rap," *AP News*, 2 May 2015).

More recently, during World War II, some folks decided to build the Alaska Highway. But they knew that whoever they sent to do the work would certainly die of the bitter cold. Who could they send? Whose lives were so disposable that . . . ? You know where I'm going with this: they sent Black people! They sent people whose origins were closer to the equator up to the bitter cold where they would certainly die. Those Black people built that highway, but they didn't die. They came back. And folks said, "See? We knew it. These aren't people. They're not like us. They have the strength of ten. They don't crack."

Okay, so what? What does any of that have to do with us here, now?

I read somewhere that if you want to cultivate an organ for transplant, the most viable non-human host is a pig, because weird science math says a pig is, somehow, three-fifths the same as a human. That means you could take a kidney out of a pig and pop it right into a person. That's fucking gross! Because pigs are filthy. That's how we think of them. Because North America is founded on Christian principles, which are in turn founded on Judaic principles, and pigs are not kosher. They're filth. It's one of the reasons cops hate being called pigs.

---

72 In 2019 my friend's name became a colloquialism for a generic white woman who embodies the privilege of whiteness (see calling cops on a park barbecue, demanding a permit for a child's lemonade stand, insisting folks speak English, asking to see the manager, etc.).

Same reason that in other parts of the world cops are more likely to be called dogs. Because in Islam, dogs are haraam—filth. Just like how in Rwanda, Tutsis were considered roaches—filth. And how in Poland, Jews were considered vermin—filth.

Oh!

I hate zombie movies. Can I talk about this for a minute? The premise of a zombie movie is this: there are beings among us who look very much like us but are distinguishable through a visibly significant feature. And if you can distinguish them from us by this visibly significant feature, then for you to slaughter them wholesale is not horrific—it's heroic.

Fuck zombies.

In 1787, the US instituted something called the Three-Fifths Compromise. Southern landowners, needing more votes to advance their interests federally, well they realized that votes are attached to people. But they didn't have any more people; they just had these . . . slaves. So they elevated the legal status of each slave to three-fifths of a person. This meant that no individual slave could go to the polls and vote in their own interest, but a slave owner could add up all the slaves he owned and vote those whole numbers.

Three fifths.

So I guess, in a roundabout way, I do understand why cops hate to be called pigs. Cuz when you call a cop a pig, you're saying he's only three fifths human. You're saying he's no more human than me. Isn't that disgusting.

But he knows he's different than me cuz, for one thing, I don't crack.

Guys, watch this. It's amazing. They don't crack. They don't crack. They don't—

the performer pounds her fist into her open palm.

BALANCE

the performer picks up the mic.

Big blue. Institutionally strong and true
I feel so safe when I see you
Sharp eyes trained on dark guys with shadowy intentions
Daily facing horrors we don't mention
It's hard and it hardens and you hardly even feel it
Going on.
Joy going, going, gone
It can't be easy.
I get that.

Still, I wish we had a body that could keep the peace
With a mandate to make hate decrease
Giving every living citizen their rights at least
These nice people could police the police

They'd have special training and be extra alert
With a prime directive:[73] nobody gets hurt
But still not afraid to go digging in the dirt

---

73   Starfleet General Order 1 prohibits interference with the other cultures and
civilizations (a prohibition violated in 110% of *Star Trek* episodes).
74   In Canada, some ten thousand immigrants are jailed monthly without charges
and incarcerated indefinitely, like Jamaican citizen Alvin Brown, who spent nearly

These frigging heroes could police the police

I wish we had a structure that was interconnected
Integrating policy with different perspectives
Empowered, impassioned, ideally elected
Those guys could help us to police the police.

If only. Oh, if only.
That's just wishful thinking

I wish we had a culture obsessed with blame
Due process,[74] assessing cases as they came
Holding people accountable and naming names.[75]
If we were like that, we would police the police.

If only there was some ever-watchful eye[76]
With cameras in hand, in your pocket, in the sky
And a code of integrity that says "don't lie"
Maybe they could take a turn and police the police

five years in immigration detention. Without citizenship status, the right to due
process does not legally extend to them (No One is Illegal—Toronto).

75   "In Canada, it is rare for police involved in fatal incidents to be officially
identified unless a criminal charge is laid . . . " (Wendy Gillis, "Should All Police

You wanna say both sides do it? Shitty.
Know who doesn't write me a paycheque? The city.
I'll do it if I have to, but you can say it with me:
It shouldn't be my job to police the police.

the performer floors the mic.

Officers Involved in Fatal Shootings be Identified?" *Toronto Star*, 3 Apr. 2017).

76   In 2018, the Toronto Police Service considered using ShotSpotter, controversial technology intended to locate and identify gunfire. Community
members concerned about state surveillance were reassured that police knew

DEATH NOTICE

Sometimes, there's so much,
I can't make sense of it, but that's not my job. My job is to tell it.
Zed's the big picture guy.

Right, Zed?
Right, Zed?

Zed?

which neighbourhoods to focus on. Many did not find this reassuring. (See
Constantine Gidaris, "How Police Surveillance Technologies Act as Tools of
White Supremacy," *Brighter World*, 13 Jan. 2020.)

TALK TO AUDIENCE FROM IN THE HOUSE

the performer leaves the stage and sits in the audience.

Hi, I'm over here, now. Because when you do a solo show, it's virtually mandatory, at some point, to break the fourth wall for intimacy. So this is that. I have something to tell you:

Once, I was a nice girl.
Then something inside me broke,
And I think it's still broken.

the performer returns to the stage.

DRINKWATER

One time, I was rehearsing for a show and Zed was watching me. My mouth was so dry I could barely get the words out.

Zed asked, "Donna, do you want some water?"

I said, "No! Water is for breaks. I'm working."

Zed said, "Donna. You want some water."

I said, "No! First you run the show, then you get your water."

Zed asked, "What do you think the show is?"

I said, "It's the thing I'm rehearsing."

Zed said, "No, Donna. The people came to see you. You're the show. If you cough, they'll watch you cough. If you do a song, they'll watch the song. If you drink your water, they'll watch you drink it, cuz that's the show. The show is whatever you do."

Zed says . . . Zed used to say, "Drink your water."

I'm going to drink my water now.

the performer raises a bottle of water, blesses Zed's hat, pours some on the floor for respeck[77] and drinks the remaining water.

---

77   It is common in hip hop culture to pour a portion of one's libation on the ground before drinking (as in Tupac Shakur's 1994 song "Pour Out a Little Liquor") as tribute to dead homies, a practise with cultural ties to ancestral reverence.

GOD IS A MURDERER

the performer picks up a mic.

My little brother[78] was a motherfucking sucker punch
Good? Boy he was good
Better than me and I'm the best[79]
So I guess he was perfect
Fucking perfect, and that's worse if you're
Nursing a grudge against God.
Which I am.

Too good to be true, so now he's not.
Too real to be here, so now he's not.
He's not.
He's . . .

My brother is dead are the worst words conceivable
Therefore unbelievable how many brothers I accumulate
Like spares
So if one dies, who fucking cares

---

78   Zaccheus Jackson (1978–2014) was an inspired and inspiring spoken word artist from the Blackfoot nation.

79   Fact.

But, opposite the plan, my growing clan only multiplies
the pangs
As my hand pours land over the lid of another casket
I'm sorry
I'm a basket case.
But at least I'm not a murderer
God is.

God is a train on a track
God is a mistimed lean back
God is a fucking hack.
I really mean that.
Smiting is so last deity.

My brother was good, but he preferred the word Nyce[80]
In spite of his life not quite living up to it
He talked fast, but it was worth learning to listen
Cuz his vision was burning
Even in prison[81] he was learning

---

80   "Blood vs Water" by Zaccheus Jackson.
81   "Wings" by Zaccheus Jackson.

He was loving this existence
He was good to go the distance
Even with us on his back
If he had to
Legs less sturdy back in the days of crack[82]
And he owned it
If he toned it down he would be lying
So he blasted
He's the one who should have lasted
Lips revealing teeth
Lungs expanded full, he's holding vapour
He'd give you his last rolling paper
If you needed it more
He'd give you mouth-to-mouth if you were bleeding disease on the floor[83]
He'd save your life at the possible price of his own
If he had to

---

82   "Recovery" by Zaccheus Jackson.

83   "Chief" by Zaccheus Jackson.

Which he didn't
But he did
Until he didn't
Until he couldn't
Until he wasn't
Until then.
When he was murdered.
By God.
Who is a murderer.
Y'heard?

Said gimme back what was taken or I'm gonna raise hell
You can't just do what you want when I am wanting as well
Sun, sea, land, air. Oh you think you're fucking clever
Who the fuck died and made you everything, ever?

I know nothing's ever gonna be the same
Things shifted when he left like they did when he came
And everyone everywhere knows who's to blame

Oh God.
God.
God.

You son of a bitch.

What,
Nothing to say?
I didn't think so.
You ain't shit.

the performer floors the mic.

PERMITS

They don't tell you that you can't play the clubs
They don't tell you anything.
They go straight to the clubs, ask to see their permits,
Express concern about the kind of acts they've been booking,
The element those acts attract.[84]
Maybe shut the place down for a day for inspection.
Maybe make it inconvenient to draw this kind of heat in the future.
So you're never actually banned anywhere.
Just, the list of places where you're welcome is dwindling.
Pretty soon we'll be back in the streets.
There's only so many clubs, you know?
But we got tonight.

So before we get the boot out the back door,[85]

Do you want more?

---

84   On New Year's Eve 2017 police were called to Blank Canvas Gallery, a Black-owned Toronto arts venue, for a noise complaint. Upon arrival, they seized the cash box and tasered owner John Samuels, who returned in the morning to find the venue padlocked, the gallery evicted.

COLLATERAL

the performer picks up the mic.

Officer, officers. This isn't about you. Is it?
Oh, you mad? You don't like my point of view?
Well if you never killed nobody, I ain't talking to you
If you never bruised a knuckle on my face, then we're cool.
Do you, man. Do blue.

It's called collateral damage.[86] Get it?
You might hurt some of the best
When you're dealing with the rest.

It's collateral damage.
You coined the term,
Now you learn what it's like.
Live with it.

So. If you're a good cop, good for you
You got some in-house cleaning to do
But I should warn you, before the next verse
It only gets worse.

---

85   In 2006, Somali Canadian rapper K'naan's manager, Sol Guy, was assaulted
and arrested in Sweden after being refused re-entry to the backstage area of the
Trädgår'n nightclub to retrieve gear immediately following a performance.
86   In 2015 Toronto Police Chief Mark Saunders dismissed the negative

Officer 44612
You see me? Huh, I see you
When you look into the mirror it's a big piece of poo
And if you think I'm playing now, wait till I get through . . .

Officer 44612, I got words for you

It's a breach of the peace when I speak of police
But I can't get a meeting with the chief of police[87]
It's really kind of rude, and I think that the least
You could do is release that name, that you know.[88]
That I know that you know.
That you know that I know that you know.
So why we playing? Oh wait, I'm not.
You'd be coughing it up like a player
If the mayor, or an MP, or an MPP made a plea
And the fact that you haven't means they haven't
Means they don't plan to.

Wait, hold on.
Hold on, what?

---

impact of carding as collateral damage—the casual violation of civil rights being
a reasonable price to pay for the negligible benefit of hypothetical leads from
confronting "random" citizens.

87 Ontario Premier Kathleen Wynne agreed to meet with Black Lives Matter

Bad apples. You got some bad apples.
Bad apples. You got some bad apples. Get 'em out.

the performer floors the mic.

Toronto activists after two weeks of protest in 2015; Chief Mark Saunders did not
comply with the meeting request.
88   For privacy reasons, law enforcement in Canada does not release the name
of the shooter in an officer-involved shooting unless charges are laid, relying on
an opaque internal process to make that determination. Say no more.

PIGDOG

Oh hey, officers. You tired of hearing "pig"? Maybe you're right.
It is getting a bit played out. Should we take a cue from brother
Weld El and switch it up? How do we feel about "dog" instead?
I'm not afraid of change.

Drop the beat.

Quick question: What's worse? A pig or a dog?
The canine or the porcine? A mutt or a hog?
Both have subhuman brains. Both can be trained, to a limited
extent.
Both can pay the rent. If you invent them to do so.
If you invest in the best of their potentials.
Both need sleep. Both cost to upkeep.
In the end both can be friends, or both can be meat
(If you are inclined to eat the four legged)
Both beg. Both will hump your leg.
Both are known to attack, run in packs and are loyal

And have served at the privilege of royals.
So what's worse, a dog or a pig?
Which are you willing to feed until it's fat and big?
Which one sleeps at the foot of your bed?
Which is more easily led?

Is it

Pig? Dog? Pig? Dog?
Both exist in filth and are prone to rage
Both eat shit, fuck their sisters
And engage in other bestial acts
They have too much muscle density to relax
Both like to hunt
One squeals, one barks, both grunt
They typically like to target the runts
The weak
The ones less likely to speak—

time stops—beat thrums.

TIME OUT

TIME OUT.

The idea of a freestyle[89] is this:
Say some shit, filter free,
Let's see how good your brain works.
The reality is,
Freestyle is freeing, but it's also exposing.
The rhyme leads you as much as the story does,
And when the words come out,
They are as much a surprise to you
As they are to anyone else.

And sometimes it's so inspired,
Like your subconscious makes in the instant
All these clear links between obscure ideas
That a night of staring at blank paper cannot command.

Sometimes nothing comes
And it's all cat, hat, bat
Throw your hands in the air
And such

---

89   Freestyle can refer to either a written rhyme that doesn't adhere to any
theme or purpose, or an improvised rhyme delivered without forethought (I use
the latter here, obvs).

90   During a 1990 resurgence of conservative decency standards, Floridian

But sometimes you open up a channel and the rhyme comes
through you.
It's a leap of faith
You start saying
And what you say sticks to you
And everyone thinks that's what you think
And they're right, you did think it
At least once
So, fair enough.

But you never know which straw is gonna be the last one
You never know when someone, somewhere decides you're a
symbol of the thing they just decided to eradicate.

You can go from nothing to everything
From not worth noticing to enemy of the people[90]
From a poet to a problem to criminal[91]
Slander, death threats, incitement to riot[92] . . .

---

lawmakers launched charges of obscenity at 2 Live Crew's album *As Nasty As They Wanna Be*. One record store owner was arrested for selling the album, while the group itself was arrested for performing their songs in Miami. It did not stick.

91 In 2012 Qatari poet Mohammed al-Ajami was given a life sentence for writing the poem "Tunisian Jasmine." This sentence, presumably, relieved the poet

THE BOY 5 – CAN'T TAKE A HINT?

Remember that boy?
He really can't take a hint.
While the little French village where he lives petitions for his
deportation,[93] he's released a video for his new song.
It's called "Dangerous"[94]
And that's his right.

Good luck to you, brother.

Good luck to us all.

---

of his impression that the emir's regime was repressive and authoritarian. .

92   According to Tunisian Prime Minister Ali Laarayedh, free speech in Tunisia
remains intact because Weld El 15's charge was "for inciting hatred and calling
for the death of police and magistrates" (Bill Chappell, "Jailed Tunisian Rapper Is
Freed; Song Called Police 'Dogs,'" *WNYC*, 2 Jul. 2013).

TIME IN

Cuz you never know exactly when that happens.
You never know when some judge is gonna sign the warrant that
makes the last loop of the noose they watch you walk into.
I mean, sometimes you know . . .

TIME IN.

They eat your sons and
They eat your daughters
It's time we take them all to the slaughter.

Pig. Dog Pig. Dog. Pig. Dog Pig.

Get your axes, get your guns
Get your bricks, get your bats
Now run, pig. Run.
KILL THE PIGS! KILL, KILL THE PIGS! KILL TH—

SMASH!

---

93 Weld El 15 was eventually expelled from France in 2018.
94 Weld El 15 featuring Phénix, "Dangereux," 2013.

BOTTLERAIN

the performer is on stage in a club, broken glass raining down from above.

Fractured sky flying
In slices of light
Shattered constellations
Kaleidoscoping crystals in
Heineken green
Red Stripe brown and Corona clean
Making me radiant
I'm bathing in hard shards
Glinting
Jewels catching in kinks
Inscribing scribbles
In (B) visible hide

Gimme the boots.
Gimme the boots.

Knowing those throwing will not be arrested
They're dressed in their Teflon
My tresses get stepped on
I'm swept on the writhing tide
Of interrupted lives
I go lizard low
Eyes knee high
Check the bottleneck,
Blocked.
Pivot
Try the next door
Textured floor
Scraping belly
Escaping hell.
He's
Not gonna get me.
Whoever he is,
I know this:
He's not going to get me.

CHASE

the performer is running through alleys.

Have you ever been chased?
I don't recommend it.

A few people chasing you because you pissed them off
Eventually run off their anger
They get tired and go home
If you evade them for long enough

A squad of people chasing you because you pissed them off
With insults
And death threats
And such
A squad of people well armed and disciplined,
Endangered,
Working in shifts

They keep chasing.
As long as they want.

And I keep thinking,
"I live for this. Don't want to die for this.[95]
I live for this. Don't want to die for this."

Until I'm breathing so hard I can't hear myself thinking it
anymore
But by then it's looping in time with my racing heart

I live for this. Don't want to die for this.
Alley. Alley. Bushes. Bridge.

I live for this. Don't want to die for this.
Train tracks. Parking lot. Jump the chain-link.

I live for this. Don't want to die for this.
Alley. Alley. Dumpster. Ditch.

Home.

the performer raises her middle finger.

---

95   In 2015 Texan Sandra Bland was taken into police custody during a "routine
traffic stop" and was found dead in her cell the next morning in what was ruled
a suicide. Video of her confrontation with the arresting officer later surfaced,
giving rise to questions that remain unanswered.

You didn't get me yet.
You didn't get me yet.
You didn't get me yet.

I say my space into being.
I raise these walls
[From bricks of conviction,
Constructing through diction
A frame at which I am the centre
And no one can enter
Whom I do not invite

Impregnable blanket fort
Whose fortitude is in my faith
I'm safe . . .]

During the above the performer hears or sees police, and falters.

STAY DOWN LOW

Stay down
If you're skittish, or petty, or need to stay pretty
If you can't move without decision by committee
If you think giving up your freedom make you safe
If you believe if you behave they won't break your face
Stay down
Stay down

the performer shakes her head, stays down.

HOME FROM THE RIOTS

This is what it's like to skip the protest.
When they say "people really came out and made a difference today,"
You know that's not you.
When they say "not many people showed up today,"
You know that is you, those gaps, they're you.
And what are you good for if other people are out there fighting your battles? But didn't I do my shift, and do you mind if I chill the fuck out and live my life for a minute, and aren't there days off in the revolution, and you already know the answer, so why are you asking. This, this knowing and not doing, it's gotta be bad for your heart.

So get up. Get up. Get up.

ALL THE NAMES, EVER

Been kept quiet so long
But the names ain't gone
We've whispered to each other down the years,
Between the bunks,
Along the assembly line,
In the mess hall, bank and barbershop
We shout silent in tattoos, tees and caps
All the platforms you cannot slap locks on
Walking bodies as monument to all of the fallen

We keep these names
Here, and here, and here
When they fade we say them over.
Every time you pave them over
We shovel up and disinter those bones
All the does, Johns and Janes, they got names
That I don't know. Shame on me, shame.

I remember you.
I can't let you be anonymous
I cannot hold all these names
I cannot know all these stories
I cannot separate the details
I can't. I can't.
I can't not try.
So let me hold your eyes, his name, her last words, their children, let me
I will hold them for as long as I can, but when I can't anymore
This goes out to all the names, ever
To all the names ever
All the names

IS IT ON?[96]

Sun's coming up on Black bodies littering the pavement
Concrete less bitter than enslavement, boss
Morning dew turned to frost
White lines on ridges
Gods dive from bridges[97]
When it isn't
Enough to be strong
Any longer
We gon' be al—[98]
And the chorus comes around again
Forty lips fuller than before
Mm mn. Follow drops that lead to the river
Mm mn. Our wounded bleed at the river
Mm mn. Predators come feed at the river
Mm mn. While we try to heal at the river
Is this on?
Is it on?

96   In 2016 a Black Lives Matter Toronto encampment occupied the entrance
to Toronto Police headquarters, demanding police release the name of the officer who fatally shot Andrew Loku. This piece commemorates that action.
97   Suicide is not uncommon among those ground down by an intractable
system, like Ohio activist MarShawn McCarrel and Kalief Browder, who was

Hoodies huddled in doorways
Four ways from Sunday
We told you that
One day we'd hold you
To account
We gon' be al—
And the chorus comes around again
Four hundred lips fuller than before
Mm mn. Cuz the verse wraps rage in the rhythm
Mm mn. And a hearse is paid to be driven.
One two, one two
Who broke the neck?
Who wrote the cheque?[99]
Is this on?
Is it on?

imprisoned for three years without conviction at the Rikers Island jail complex in New York—two of those years in solitary confinement.

98   This chanted lyric from "Alright" by Kendrick Lamar animated activists at the Black Lives Matter Toronto encampment in joyful solidarity.

99   In the six years following Michael Brown's death at the hands of police, six

MOVE IT ALONG

I'm down at Pride, taking it in before taking the stage later in
the afternoon, and it's really hot. It's hot and I'm sloppy so I
go in search of one of the city's three trees. Just off the corner
of Church and Wellesley, I pass the Wine Rack where they are
perpetually giving out free samples, and everyone is on the sidewalk drinking and milling and taking off their pants and dancing
if they want to, because the rules are temporarily suspended
when we feel festive. There's the tree, and there's no one under
it because people who live here are like "what's that thing?" and
all the tourists come from places that have more than three. So
I sit in the shade, and after a couple of minutes a couple of guys
come and sit beside me. We're just sitting. And a couple of cops
come over and they say to the guys,

"Okay, move it along."

Ferguson, Missouri, activists have turned up dead, while others have received
credible threats.

And the guys get up like they're gonna do that, so I get up too.
I'm like, "Where should we go?"

And he says, "I wasn't talking to you."

Which is weird, right? Cuz there are three of us sitting there.
And I realize I am sitting near people who make me look less
dangerous on the curve.
I realize that today I am one of the people for whom the rules
are suspended, but these guys, they are not. That they are actually being moved along for me, for the tourists, for our festivity.
That this cop has decided he can distinguish me from them in
some "significant" way that means they have to move on and I
get to stay.

Get up. Get up. Get up.

So I'm like, "Where should we go?"

And he says, "I wasn't talking to you."

And I say, "You are now."
And he turns to face me, because he is now.

He says, "Who are you?"

And I understand that for him, there is a right answer, one that extracts me from the situation, one that makes it obvious that I am not with these guys, and I flip through my adjectives to guess what it might be.

Is my post-secondary degree pinned to my two-inch shorts?

Is it the pigmental difference between my lightly toasted and their burnt sienna?

Is it my unenviable absence of phallus?

Is it the fact that I don't appear to be carrying all my worldly possessions?

He says, "Who are you?"

And I guess I lose my fucking mind, cuz I say,

"Who am I?
I'm a secret agent.
I'm a fried egg.
I'm Margaret Thatcher.
I'm none of your fucking business!
Because whoever I am has a right to stand here
Whoever I am has a right to speak here
Whoever I am can take off my pants and dance if I want to,
And so can they, whoever they are . . .
I'm with them, whoever they are . . .
Who am I?
I'm people.
They're people.
And you?
You're rude."

LONDON CALLING

the performer picks up the mic.

Somebody, somewhere is getting a call[100]
Because there is something that connects us all
It's a need to believe we'll be saved somehow
And I need to believe more than ever right now
(B)(B) I been known to say some shit
And I more or less expect to get away with it
Could I still be vocal with a gun to me?
If I was far away in prison, would you come for me?
If I don't make the headlines, how will you know?

Somebody, somewhere's on the phone.
London calling. London calling.
And somebody somewhere can never go home.
London calling. London calling.

---

100   This song was written to acknowledge the work of Marilyn McKim, whose role in Urgent Action at Amnesty International Canada involves mobilizing escalated advocacy for urgent cases assigned by the organization's head office in London. This also references the Clash's 1979 song of the same name.

This is more than beating on a drum for me
If you speak for the imprisoned then you done for me
You carry a weight that's like a ton for me
Keep forgotten names on your tongue for me
There are people who survive because you name them
Powers that do right because you shame them
Compassion is good, but it's just motivation.
Cars need engines. Movements need mobilization.
Movements need people who actually do
Inspire, ignite, unify and follow through
Eat on the picket line, sleep in your shoes
To the people in the front, merci beaucoup
For all those who stand with our stolen sisters[101]
For being steadfast, tireless and persistent
For getting the backs of those on their last legs
For ringing the alarm, and waking the dead
For saying, even in solitary,[102] you are not alone.

Somebody somewhere is on the phone.
London calling. London calling.
And somebody somewhere can never go home.
London calling. London calling.

---

101   Stolen Sisters: the Canadian epidemic of Missing and Murdered
Indigenous Women and Girls.
102   A Thunder Bay prison held Adam Capay for over 1,600 days in solitary
confinement—significantly in excess of the fifteen-day maximum set out by the
United Nations.

I used to say
I'm doing what I can and I'm better than most
I mean I'm pretty damned nice, I don't like to boast
I got one for you and forty-two for me
I ain't trying to get over, I'm just trying to get free
Not jealous of my knowledge, just too busy to teach
Never turn a blind eye, but a look ain't a reach
These my shoes. This my walk.
Yours ain't mine. Tough love. True talk.
I am an us and it's rough for them
Yeah, I think about it now and then.
When I leak free speech from the tip of my pen
And polite bite back is the consequence
But anyone who's been there knows
You're at the edge of the precipice before you see how deep it
goes . . .

London calling. London calling.
London calling. Somebody's getting disappeared
He's been sitting in darkness for three years
Tell him he's not forgotten.
Remember his name.
London calling.

CYPHER

The cypher is a circle,
Like a sacred congregation
Of spontaneous exchange,
Ideas and energy the same
In that we're sparking from the flame
Of this engagement,
Relegated to the basements
Unpremeditated
And extemporaneous.

Welcome.

the performer turns the mic outward, fist up. Lights fade to Black.

"end"

WHAT IS RADICAL EMPATHY?
BY ANDY MCKIM

Donna-Michelle St. Bernard's plays shine a light on the over-looked stories of our generation. Both poetic and lean, and deploying the power of metaphor, imagery and allegory, her plays revolve around large-scale actions that are playing themselves out within our communities or even across the globe—more like parables than naturalistic drama. And yet each play takes on a different character. I think this is because Donna-Michelle doesn't believe her plays are finished until they have been produced in collaboration with a creative team. Those artists help her to unlock all of the latent evocative power that lies within her spare writing. She relies on her collaborators to put the interpretive "meat on the bone."

Sound of the Beast is different. Donna-Michelle chose to write about her very specific lived experience as a Black womxn and a Black artist. The play powerfully evokes Donna-Michelle's experience of "our peculiar ways"—a Canadian euphemism for racism. Without Donna-Michelle's testimony in this play, some of us might be unaware of the depth and breadth of the everyday racism that she encounters. Or for those who are deeply familiar with her lived experience, the play acts as a powerful affirmation of their own history of being marginalized. Either way, the audience's engagement with *Sound of the Beast* can be transformational.

Dramatic stories like these give us a chance to learn from someone else's unique experience of our world. One of the antecedents of modern theatre is the age-old desire to hear a compelling story from someone who has had a unique experience.

For one early example of this I look to ancient Greek the-atre, which is often thought of as the most important forerunner of Eurocentric theatrical storytelling. While I acknowledge the importance of Sophocles, I have always been inspired by Pheidippides. He was the soldier chosen to run twenty-five miles from the battlefield at Marathon to alert the people in Athens to the news that the battle had been won. He is reported to have run the entire distance, without stopping, until he could finally storm into the Assembly to share the news . . . at which point he collapsed and died. Not only was he the inspiration for today's "marathon" race, but I have to think that his report of the victory on that battlefield must have been both the most dramatically powerful and relevant story that the people in Athens had ever witnessed. It was storytelling at its finest. And it inspires us to situate the most powerful stories in our world within the immediacy of an intimate theatre experience.

With *Sound of the Beast* we see Donna-Michelle storm into the theatre and tell us what is happening in the streets. As audience members, we play the role of her community and that implicates us in what she is saying.

Jiv and I (as co-dramaturges/directors), along with Donna-Michelle, were initially focused on which elements of *Sound of the Beast* were central to the story and which ones were peripheral. What became clear to us over time is that the more the play focused on Donna-Michelle's voice and experience, the more powerful it became. In the beginning of the writing process, Donna-Michelle had created a fictional character who was at the centre of the piece. Over time we realized that this fictional character needed to be cut in favour of foregrounding Donna-Michelle and her lived experience. She needed to be speaking as herself in her own voice. While Donna-Michelle the playwright was fine with this shift, Donna-Michelle the actor was not. But I was convinced that the authenticity of her direct engagement with an audience would be much more powerful than any "performance."

I had always been interested in how personal this play was compared to her other plays, and I had always been convinced that the more vulnerable, more honest and the more personable Donna-Michelle was with the audience, the more powerful their experience would be. But this was a difficult challenge. Donna-Michelle was not entirely comfortable performing as herself in a theatrical context, telling her own stories. Compounding this situation, her impulse to tell Weld El 15's story made the pivot to her personal experiences even more challenging. However, this balance between source material and embodied knowledge arises throughout Donna-Michelle's 54ology of plays, which are all inspired by (but rarely depicting) continental African stories.

It is almost always difficult for a writer to know exactly what sort of beast their play is until they see it staged. In the case of this "Beast," it was additionally challenging to know exactly what this play was—in advance of production—because it was not written using a linear narrative.

Donna-Michelle had many ambitions with this work, and when it first appeared before the public it was a vast, sprawling, ambitious piece of theatre. In the time since that first public performance in April 2017, the script/production has changed a great deal, mainly because a quarter of the text has been cut.

Once we agreed that all of the text should somehow be related to oppression and/or marginalization, we were able to cut a lot of material using this guideline to make the play's trajectory more focused. We liked what this did to the piece, and Donna-Michelle felt that this more focused story was what she wanted to communicate. (You'll find that some of the cut material is included in this published version of the play.)

Donna-Michelle's performances in the play were constantly feeding back into the writing of the play, which was a unique experience for her. Each night she found it extremely difficult to be speaking so directly and frankly to an audience. Would her stories, her tone, alienate an audience. Did it matter if they did? Wasn't that the point?

I was certain that if she took good care of the audience, as a performer, then her empathy for us would allow us to open up to her truth. I think it is important to be emotionally honest with an audience in the theatre and with people in our lives. It would be fair to say that both Donna-Michelle and I are guarded people—in part, because it can be dangerous to be too vulnerable. But together with Jiv we were able to forge a performance for Donna-Michelle that was based on opening up to the audience, treating them with respect . . . which created the opportunity for each of us, along with the audiences, to go to the more difficult, or vulnerable, places.

Andy McKim focuses his professional life on developing, dramaturging, directing and producing new Canadian plays. He was recently Artistic Director of Theatre Passe Muraille (2007–2019), and was Associate Artistic Director of Tarragon Theatre (1986–2007), where he created and programmed the Spring Arts Fair. Andy was President of the Professional Association of Canadian Theatres (2002–2005) and President of the Toronto Theatre Alliance (1997–1999). Among other awards, Andy has been recognized with the Playwrights Guild of Canada's Bra D'or Award (for playwright gender equity), the George Luscombe Mentorship Award and the Dora Mavor Moore Silver Ticket Award for Lifetime Achievement.

Now here's a likkle truth
Open up your eye
While you're checking out the boom-bap, check the exercise
Take the word "overseer," like a sample
Repeat it very quickly in a crew for example
Overseer
Overseer
Overseer
Overseer
Officer, Officer, Officer, Officer!
Yeah, officer from overseer
You need a little clarity?
Check the similarity!
—KRS-One, "Sound of da Police"

I always struggle to give context to the words of poets. Any essay seems to fail to take in the breadth of the scope and experience they bring through their art form. But I'm gonna do it anyway!

What I love about that KRS-One verse is how, at least to me, once you say it—once you feel your mouth navigate the words "overseer/officer," you can't undo it. It points to a lineage of policing throughout history. Like many people, perhaps you as well, my ancestors were subject to the discipline and punitive authority of the "overseer" on the plantation. But the overseer was not the one in charge—they were middle management. In Trinidad the overseers were often Scottish—lesser status than the British—but higher status than the Indians, Africans, Asians and Indigenous peoples. Perhaps an overly compassionate view of these overseers could see a person entrapped in a larger machine of oppression for the growth of an empire that was simultaneously occupying and displacing them from their own land. Sending them across the ocean to enact colonial violence similar to what they would be subject to in their own home. But even in that compassionate gaze, over the shoulder—gazing at the overseer with the whip and cane—it doesn't change the fact of the fear and intimidation exercised through the lash.

Modern policing similarly operates as that arm of the landowner. Only the landowner is replaced by the collective democratic landowners, "the people." Under the pretense of a safer society, we maintain a system of middle management of civic order—the arm of the state. And again, a compassionate view of police officers can see that, in reality, many police officers have come to their profession and duty through life circumstances rather than an abundance of choice. Including my family. My brother's a cop. And some of my best friends growing up are now cops. These people who I love deeply have entered the middle management of civic society—and I'd be lying if I said it wasn't complicated. But still, it doesn't change the fact of the fear and intimidation exercised through a slow cruise, a random stop and search or riot horses on a Saturday night. When you find yourself enwrapped in a gaze as somewhat "shifty"—or fitting a profile—you reflect back a gaze that sees danger. Maybe it's irrational, but rationality and emotional truth rarely tend to live harmoniously together.

But is this news to you? Would giving statistics on the disproportionate policing of marginalized communities really tell you anything you didn't already know? I doubt it—after all, you just picked up a play called *Sound of the Beast*—which, given, could be a Christian epic (not saying it's not). That's where art comes in. That's where writing about these everyday real issues in a removed analytical sense, it just fails to compare. But in sequencing an emotional throughline of embodied thought, maybe there's some insight into the experience of being enwrapped in a gaze; maybe there's some coded identification if you live with it. Poets do it better.

As part of Donna-Michelle's 54ology—one project for each country in continental Africa—this project took its inspiration from the case of Weld El 15, an emcee who was persecuted and forced into exile for his ability to speak truth to power. The same skills were utilized to disavow an old regime and get new politicians into power only to have the arm of the state turn against him when he didn't fall in line by looking past how little had changed in this new order.

The reason I'm actually writing to you now is that Donna-Michelle asked me to talk about my contributions in the process of the creation of this piece. And beyond offering some thoughts on where to stand and the overall structure—let's not make direction seem like a lofty auteurism after all—my contributions were this kind of perspective that I've been writing about. Being somewhere in a spectrum of a conflicted relationship with authority, policing, generational resistance. A perspective that, while there are overlaps with my colleagues in the room, is distinct. Distinct from Andy, Rebecca, David, Heather, Cam, Donna-Michelle—all the collaborators that fed into what this piece became. The benefit of bringing these perspectives together was to identify the codes at play within the poetry. There are things that one of us could take for granted, that another would not; there are things that needed no explanation for some of us as just the reality we exist in and were devastating to understand for others. I'll put it this way—I read a story about a new function on Apple's Siri app where you could say "Siri, I'm being pulled over" and the app then switches to silent mode, sends a text message to select contacts notifying them you are being pulled over and begins recording. For some of us in the room it was so sad that the function had to exist. For me at least it was brilliant. Enough so that I spent the next hour trying to program an automated feature into my Android phone to do the same. Yes, I use Android. Because I have problems with authority. And I could go on about the things I somehow learned about de-escalation, where my hands go when talking to a police officer, my reaction to a gunshot—cuz I didn't grow up on the "rough streets." I grew up on a cul-de-sac in Dartmouth, Nova Scotia, in Mi'kma'ki —but some things you just know. Some codes just make sense. It's somewhere bridging rational and irrational, and as much as I can try to tease it out here, there's really no point. Cuz poets say it better.

Jivesh Parasram is an award-winning multidisciplinary artist of Indo Caribbean descent (Cairi/Trinidad & Tobago). Jivesh grew up in Mi'kma'ki (Nova Scotia) before moving to Tkaronto (Toronto). In 2009 he co-founded Pandemic Theatre, through which much of his work has been created, often in close collaboration with co-founder Tom Arthur Davis. He is a recipient of two Harold Awards for his service to the independent theatre community in Tkaronto, including the Ken McDougall Award. Jivesh won the 2018 Toronto Arts Foundation Emerging Artist Award, and was a member of the second cohort of the Cultural Leaders Lab with the Toronto Arts Council and the Banff Centre. In 2018, Jivesh took on the position of artistic director for Rumble Theatre. He lives primarily in the unceded Coast Salish territories (Vancouver, BC).

RECOMMENDED READING

Cole, Desmond. *The Skin We're In: A Year of Black Resistance and Power*, Penguin Random House, 2020.

Diverlus, Rodney, Sandy Hudson, and Syrus Marcus Ware, eds., *Until We Are Free: Reflections on Black Lives Matter Canada*, University of Regina Press, 2020.

Maynard, Robyn. *Policing Black Lives*, Fernwood, 2017.

Walcott, Rinaldo, and Idil Abdillahi, *BlackLife: Post-BLM and the Struggle for Freedom*, ARP Books, 2019.

ACKNOWLEDGEMENTS

Dramaturgy by Andy McKim and Jivesh Parasram. Developed with support from the Banff Centre's Spoken Word Program, the Ontario Arts Council and as Theatre Passe Muraille's Emcee in Residence. Thanks for contributions from Jazz Kamal (a.k.a. Nari), Adam Booth, Daniel Thau-Eleff, Gerard Harris, Clare Preuss, Pamela Gilmartin and Kern Albert. In the making, I was moved by the stories of Weld El 15, Parole, El Général, El Haqed, Ikram Ben Said, Pussy Riot, Tiny Doo, Igor Stravinsky and Arya Aramnejad.

Donna-Michelle St. Bernard is an emcee, playwright and arts administrator. Her work has been recognized with a Siminovitch Prize nomination, SATAward nomination, the Herman Voaden Playwriting Award, the Enbridge playRites Award, a Dora Mavor Moore Award for Outstanding New Play, and two nominations for the Governor General's Literary Award for Drama. She is the current artistic director of New Harlem Productions. She is based in Toronto.

First edition: August 2020
Printed and bound in Canada by Imprimerie Gauvin, Gatineau

Jacket photo by Graham Isador
Author photo © Denise Grant

PLAYWRIGHTS
CANADA PRESS

202-269 Richmond St. W.
Toronto, ON
M5V 1X1

416.703.0013
info@playwrightscanada.com
www.playwrightscanada.com
@playcanpress